AN Intext TEXTBOOK IN ART AND ART EDUCATION

emphasis:ART

A QUALITATIVE ART PROGRAM FOR THE ELEMENTARY SCHOOL

Book design and color photography by Frank Wachowiak. Supplemental photography by Ted Ramsay, David Hodge, W. Robert Nix, and James Kent.

Group mural "The Jungle," grade 2. Background constructed of two 4' x 8' thick-ply cardboard panels coated with black latex paint. Each youngster in class contributed a colored construction paper animal or bird which was stapled to the board. Children who finished first created additional trees, foliage, and flowers.

emphasis: ART

SECOND EDITION

A QUALITATIVE ART PROGRAM FOR THE ELEMENTARY SCHOOL

FRANK WACHOWIAK
Professor of Art
The University of Georgia

THEODORE RAMSAY
Associate Professor of Art
University of Michigan

INTEXT EDUCATIONAL PUBLISHERS
Scranton   Toronto   London

Copyright ©, 1971, by International Textbook Company

All rights reserved. No part of the material protected by this copyright notice may be reproduced or utilized in any form or by any means, electronic or mechanical, including photocopying, recording, or by any informational storage and retrieval system, without written permission from the copyright owner. Printed in the United States of America. Library of Congress Catalog Card Number: 71-152648. International Standard Book Number 1-7002-2360-6.

To children everywhere who make the teaching of art a never-ending adventure and to their teachers who share in the wonder and discovery.

PREFACE

When *Emphasis: Art* was originally written, its aim was to provide elementary school teachers with qualitative, yet realistic, art education guidelines and objectives; with proven, imaginative art teaching strategies; and with evaluative clues and criteria that could give purpose, scope, structure, and continuity to art programs in the elementary schools.

The response to the first edition has been unanimously approving. Classroom and special art teachers, art consultants, and curriculum coordinators from coast to coast have welcomed it enthusiastically. College and university art education instructors have praised its clarity, brevity, and design. Its practicability and its emphasis on the qualitative, in-depth art experience have received warm endorsement.

This second edition is the result of continuing studies and action research in the elementary schools. Art teaching strategies, techniques, and evaluative procedures based on actual classroom experiences and on observations of exemplary elementary school art practices both in this country and abroad are described in detail. A new chapter has been added dealing with continuity and sequential learning experiences in elementary art providing material that should prove significantly valuable to the classroom teacher who wants specific help in planning a developmental art curriculum.

Although a number of new discoveries and techniques are documented, the basic substance of the original text has not been altered. What gave the first edition its qualitative character remains. The book still concerns itself with the adventures, the joys, and the responsibilities of teaching art to children; with the significant, guiding role of the teacher; with art projects based on strong aesthetic foundations; and with those important evaluative clues that can help the teacher identify and nurture the art in children's art.

Emphasis: Art is recommended as a guide for elementary classroom teachers who need tangible help in planning and enriching their art programs. It is suggested as an inspiring textbook for the college student in search of a candid and unequivocal blueprint of high calibre, in-depth, elementary school art practices. In addition, it offers a straightforward description of a proven, practical program for those veteran artist-teachers who seek continuing challenges, new techniques, and classroom-tested projects for their instructional repertoire.

The importance of the instructor's influence is underscored throughout the text. The premise is clear. A creative, confident teacher, with a love of children and a growing understanding of dynamic art and design concepts, is the prime catalyst in the development of a qualitative art program. A major and significant factor in the success of any elementary art program is the unselfish, dedicated, and committed involvement of the teacher. Constant planning, thinking, dreaming, organizing, adapting, researching, experimenting, motivating, evaluating, and resource-building are the challenging and often enervating responsibilities of successful teaching today. The privilege, however, of sharing the contagious, unique exuberance of children as they discover and create, and of seeing the exciting world of color and design through a child's eyes, is worth many times the extra concern a teacher displays.

With *turned-on* teachers to guide them, children from the first through the sixth grade will respond and grow in a program where art fundamentals and techniques are not left to chance but taught systematically, imaginatively, sequentially, and purposefully. The harangue concerning process versus product is colored with ambiguities. Perceptive teachers know that wherever and whenever the *process* of discovery and creation is founded on an appreciation and utilization of art and design principles, the *product* will reflect the effects of this understanding. Mounting evidence proves that we have been underestimating the expressive capacities of children, and, in too many instances, have not fully tapped their artistic potential.

The purposes and objectives of the art program in our elementary schools demand constant re-evaluation and re-appraisal in light of the growth in other subject matter areas. Concerned professionals in art and art education have been explicit in directing attention to the growing emasculation of the visual arts in the schools, but few have proposed anything more than theoretical and unrealistic alternatives. What teachers of elementary school art need are some clear directives, some tangible specifics that can help take the mystery out of teaching art to children. This text is hopefully a step in that direction.

The philosophy, the strategy of guiding youngsters as they express themselves visually, which is documented in this book, is the hallmark of those schools where the *emphasis* is on ART, art as an adventure, a science, and a discipline with its own singular skills, its own unique core of learnings, and its own incomparable rewards.

Whatever qualitative aspects this text may possess is in no small measure due to the expressive magic of those children whose creations sparkle across the pages and to the teachers who helped make the art class a dynamic, growing experience for them.

Dr. W. Robert Nix, Professor of Art, The University of Georgia, gave generously of his time and expertise in the photographing and processing of the black and white illustrations. David Hodge, Director of Art, Campus School, University of Wisconsin-Oshkosh, provided a wealth of inspiring visual material. Mary Hammond, Art Consultant, Madison County Schools, Danielsville, Georgia, graciously al-

lowed the documentation of a number of high-calibre art projects by children in her classes. Masachi Shimono of Nihon Bunkyo Shuppan, publishers of *Arts and Crafts, A Handbook for Elementary School Children,* Osaka, Japan, gave kind permission to use illustrative material.

The authors are indebted to Lamar Dodd, Head, Department of Art, The University of Georgia, Athens, for his continued support and understanding.

Others who contributed include Ron Arnholm, Ruth Beatty, Betty Cabin, Richard Capes, Carol Collins, Carolyn Farr, Virginia Hall, Katherine Harrison, Nancy Hooten, Jim Kent, F. W. Kent, Mineo Kozuma, Mary McCutchen, Keiichi Mori, Jimmy Morris, and Helen Westbrook.

A sincere note of appreciation goes to Mr. Gerald Stashak, Vice President, International Textbook Company, and to his staff, especially to John A. Wargo, in charge of production.

FRANK WACHOWIAK
THEODORE RAMSAY

Athens, Georgia
January, 1971

CONTENTS

emphasis: ART

A QUALITATIVE ART PROGRAM FOR THE ELEMENTARY SCHOOL

1

INTRODUCTION

The teaching of art in the elementary school today is a richly rewarding and a highly fulfilling experience when it is done with conviction, purpose, planning, understanding, and love. It is a privilege, a revelation, and a joy to observe and work with children as they create in paint, crayon, pastel, clay, wood, yarn, cloth, paper, and *found materials*. Their imagination and inventiveness know no bounds; their designs and colors are excitingly unpredictable. No wonder, then, that their intuitive, naive, visual expressions have entranced and even influenced such noted painters as Henri Matisse and Paul Klee! To watch a child develop in drawing and painting skills, to see him grow from year to year in his artistic expression, is to witness a most fascinating aspect of human and individual growth. Yet this same youngster, deprived of the guidance and encouragement of a sympathetic, knowledgeable teacher, may stay on the same developmental plateau for years. His store of visual resources, his command of the vocabulary and language of art, his understanding of line, shape, form, color, pattern, texture, design, and composition may remain static or even retrogress, leading eventually to his discouragement, frustration, and apathy.

Enriched and stimulated by a teacher's varied and challenging motivations, the child learns to see more, to sense more, to recall more, to be more vitally aware of his expanding and changing environment and consequently to be able to express himself visually with more confidence. The teacher of art in the elementary school can begin talking very early to the young child about the exciting possibilities and wonders of design and color. Today's child is more inquisitive, more alert and often more discerning than his predecessors.

Inspiration for children's drawings is often as near as the school door, the view from a classroom window, a butterfly collection shared with the class. Encourage looking, feeling, and drawing from the first grade on.

1

Primary school teachers may have to rely on simpler teaching strategies, providing more easily assimilated art terminology for the children, but they will soon discover that children understand quite readily the ideas of using dark and light or dull and bright colors for contrast, of creating big and little shapes for variety, of repeating a shape or color to achieve pattern, and of drawing things large to fill the page. It is the teacher's responsibility to help build the child's creative confidence by guiding him as he moves from one art learning stage to another toward the attainment of discriminating design awareness, repeating when necessary those art principles than can bolster his visual expression and give purpose to his performance.

Teachers have been misled too often by the false assumption that anything a child draws, paints, or constructs is "art." It may be, indeed, a child's visual statement, but it is not necessarily a work of art. To be art, it must, as far as possible, be expressed in the language, structure, or form of art. Children who express their responses, their ideas, and their reactions with feeling and sensitivity and in a framework of compositional design create *art*. For the majority of children this sense of design, of art structure, of aesthetic form, must come from the many planned art experiences and practices provided by the teacher. Sometimes this knowledge can be augmented and reinforced by visits to art centers and museums and by exposure to choice art books, reproductions, films and periodicals (see Appendices C and D).

2

Very often what some observers call art in a child's drawing is not art at all but simply a visual statement that relates more to basic writing. Art, on the other hand, is more akin to poetry, which approximating fine art, comes to life when it distills the essence of things in expressive and discriminative choices. A basic statement, such as "I live in a house," might be compared, for example, to a stereotyped drawing of a boxlike house in the middle of a page. If we asked a child to tell us where he lives in a poetic way, he might say:

> My house is sunny white with a red roof
> It peeks through two big willow trees
> And a blue door in front says, "Come in."
>
> A green bush hedge goes all around my house,
> And red and yellow tulips hug the porch
> Where I sit on a swing and say, "Come in."

In much the same manner, poetic style enlivens and enriches the child's visual expression when he calls upon his store of perception, awareness, and eidetic imagery for his drawing. The house then changes from the common boxlike stereotype in the middle of the page to a highly personal place, individual and unique. It may be a house of textured brick, rough stone, clapboard, redwood, cedar shingles, or cast cement, with chimneys, shutters, iron railings, breezeways, carports, windvanes, trellises, creeping vines, lantern posts, picture windows, rock gardens, pierced screens, television antennae, molded cornices, picket fences, window flower boxes, winding driveways, cobblestoned walks, or sculptured hedges.

The child who is challenged to a perceptive awareness of his environment draws his home in a personal, individual style, emphasizing those features that make it different and unique. The children devoted several hours to these drawings.

In poetry, we discover that the quality of the interpretation often depends on the utilization of an expressive word or phrase, on effective alliteration, on accent, on meter or rhythm, and sometimes on rhyme. In the best, the most colorful art creations of children, one discerns a corollary employment of art principles and fundamentals resulting in a unity and design that distinguishes them from the ordinary, impoverished statement.

In every art guide we find an emphasis on the teacher's responsibility to help youngsters engage in worthwhile experiences in order that they may have something meaningful to express, draw, paint, print, sculpt, or construct. Sometimes the teachers help the children recall a past event or impression. More often they provide a new enrichment through a field trip, a model brought to class, a dramatization, a film, a dance, a musical recording, a story, or a poem. But for qualitative teaching in art, this initial stimulation is not enough. The teacher must also learn to guide and to counsel the children as they work, helping them to express their reactions and their responses in a growing, artistic framework.

Every time a child creates a work of art, a painting, a collage, a print, or a sculpture he should be encouraged to evaluate his effort from stage to stage in the process. If nothing is said to the growing youngster about design, structure, composition, line, value, color, texture, pattern, and other aspects of the visual art form, it is presumptuous to assume he will develop in aesthetic awareness.

4

These watercolor paintings reveal that these children were not content with stereotyped, shorthand descriptions of a place or event. Instead they combined sensitive perception and recall together with in-depth art skills to prove again how much they really see and respond to.

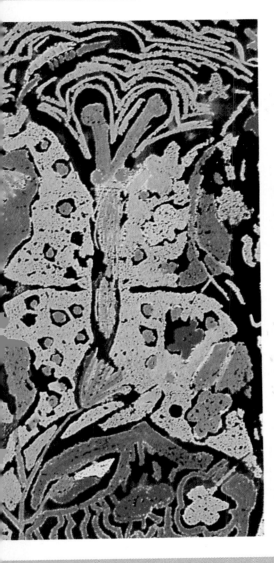

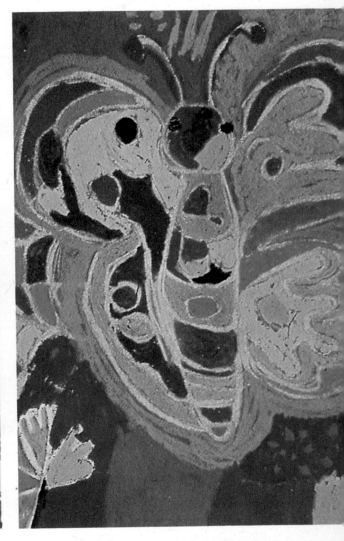

For many youngsters the classroom teacher is the most important catalyst in providing inspirational motivations for art. Children cannot create out of a vacuum. The teacher must help enrich the child's world, introducing those visual resources that can trigger exciting visual expression. The children who created these butterfly paintings did not "just draw them out of their heads." LEFT—Black tempera paint over oil pastel. Grade 3. RIGHT—Oil pastel on colored construction paper. Grade 2, Barnett Shoals School, Athens, Georgia.

5

We are surfeited with the reassurances of art educators and child psychologists who insist that it is easy to teach art to children. They speak of "the relatively little effort required" or tell us that "to be creative, children need only materials and a place to work."

Let's keep the record straight. Art is not easy to teach; that is, if we are speaking about a bona fide art class and not a play session. It requires as much preparation, intelligence, and organizational skill as any other subject area in the school and, in certain instances, even more. The teacher's expertise is a major factor in the implementation of a quality art program.

The child who draws, paints, prints, or constructs will create more fulfilling, more exciting art when he is guided to see more, to notice more, and to be more aware of his environment. If his contact with the world, with nature, is superficial, if he only half-sees its possibilities, if his identification with the visual stimulus is minimal, then he is apt to be content with a casual shorthand statement of an experience or event. Stereotyped interpretations such as stick figures, lollypop trees, square houses with triangle roofs, or two ovals for a cat's or bird's body are seldom based on a truly perceived, richly observed experience.

6

Guide the children to turn often to nature and her myriad shapes, forms, and colors for continuous inspiration in art. Nowhere are the elements of variety within unity so beuatifully evident.

The teacher must be constantly resourceful, prepared to help the child respond more fully, to react more sensitively, and to distinguish identifying characteristics more readily and effectively. This aspect of teacher guidance is only one part of the complex job of motivation but without it the average child's visual expressions tend to be cursory and sterile.

Teachers are often cautioned against imposing adult standards on children's expressive efforts. This admonition is understandable and commendable. However, there are some important standards based on aesthetic considerations that the teacher may and should use as valid evaluative criteria. These have to do with design and compositional factors, with basic art structure concepts. They range from simple, understandable guidelines in the primary grades to complex and challenging injunctions in the upper grades (see Chapter 5).

Qualitative art experiences should have an undisputed and significant place in the total curriculum of the elementary school. When art is allotted insufficient time in the school's schedule, when it plays a subordinate role to every other subject in the classroom, when it consists mainly of peripheral art activities such as chart or map making, stereotyped holiday decorations, and endless posters, it is presumptuous to expect it to perform a vital role in the expressive, personal growth of each child. Art in the elementary school is justified as long as it contributes effectively and purposefully to the aesthetic, perceptive, discriminative, and creative growth of every child. Art taught effectively has a body of knowledge and skills to be mastered. It has unquestioned merit as a unique avenue to mental, social and individual growth through creative action, and should be welcomed as a living, learning experience in its own right.

An unfortunate handicap to the implementation of a quality elementary art program is the continued employment of duplicated patterns and of misguided correlation practices wherein art is used to make the other school subjects more palatable. In the process, however, the child's love for creative, expressive art can be easily jeopardized.

Reports of art lessons and projects in art education periodicals often lead readers to believe that teachers of the art lesson are afraid to voice their true convictions, to admit that they are influencing the students in their classrooms. Yet any intelligent, perceptive, and experienced school teacher can ascertain after observing the products of child art, either in an exhibit or as illustrations in a publication, whether an instructor's creative, guiding hand was at work, no matter how many times the article or exhibit brochure insists that the children made all the decisions and all the choices. It is unfortunate, indeed, that so many teachers of art classes in our schools today are afraid to say "I teach!" Art does have content. It has a vocabulary. It has a language. Let's teach it!

Unless a person has actually taught a class of thirty or more children in today's rapidly changing schools, it is almost impossible to say what can or cannot be accomplished in art. Frequently we hear from professors long absent from the contemporary elementary school climate advising teachers to "give the child materials and let him alone to create" or "teach the child, not the subject" or "remember that it's the process not the product that is important." How easily these admonitions roll off the tongue! Classroom teachers, however, need more than generalizations today. They need specific help. Teachers faced with today's overloaded classes and schedules do well indeed if they simply keep the youngsters in control. Permissive philosophies will not solve their problems. Teachers can maintain an effective, positive, and productive equilibrium in their classes as long as they can bring the students to sense the purpose, the satisfaction in the art endeavor, and the serious direction of the effort. When youngsters realize that they are not growing in art, not develop-

ing in the mastery of art skills, processes, techniques, and knowledge, they lose interest and the critical problems of student and class control are compounded. An art class where the teacher "lets the child do as he pleases" is usually a class where a minimum of qualitative effort and progress takes place.

Teachers of elementary art can learn much, of course, from specialists in other fields. Psychologists, behavioral researchers, sociologists, anthropologists, and curriculum co-ordinators can help them augment their teaching strategies, but *ultimately it is the emphasis teachers put on art that matters, teaching it dynamically, conscientiously, and purposefully so that the children placed in their charge will grow day by day, year by year in awareness to life, in sensitivity to their changing world, in creative potential, in the ability to make worthwhile aesthetic choices, and in the appreciation of man's contribution through his art.*

In this expressive opaque watercolor painting by a young Greek child he tells us all we need to know about his world. We see it through his eyes—the sea, the village, the mountain, the winding road, the forest, the orchards, the harvesters, and, of course, the ubiquitous sun—that wonderful sun that shines in almost every very young child's painting. Long may it shine!

9

2

THE CHILD AND HIS ENVIRONMENT

Children everywhere have much in common. They react in similar ways to their environment. They laugh. They cry. They delight in seeing and manipulating bright, colorful objects. They respond to sympathetic voices and loving hands.

Children everywhere draw in almost the same manner at similar developmental stages, at corresponding age levels. They begin with haphazard scribbles, gradually acquire more control, then move to simple, geometric symbols, and finally to characteristic and semirealistic interpretations. Their natural graphic responses are generally instinctive and intuitive, yet these basic representations do not necessarily mean that they are making artistic choices. What they express so spontaneously is usually done with an unconscious naïveté.

No two children are exactly alike. Even twins, who may confuse their teachers with surface similarities, may have different personalities, different reactions and feelings, and different mental abilities. These individual, unique characteristics of children present teachers with some of their most critical guiding challenges. Teachers soon learn that they cannot expect the same responses, the same skills, or the same interpretations from any two children, even though they may be of the same age.

Children in the same class may have diverse interests and different needs. They should have an opportunity to participate in a variety of art experiences or projects in order to achieve a rewarding measure of success in some particular technique. The youngster who excels in clay manipulation may respond less

Children often live in a special world half-way between make-believe and reality. Their art is the happy result of seeing, imagining, and knowing. Teachers can help their students grow in seeing and perceiving by providing varied visual stimuli. An aquarium in the classroom or a visit to a natural museum may prove the inspiration for an oil pastel such as the one illustrated at left. Grade 4, Athens, Georgia. Circle photo: Courtesy Eastern Airlines.

enthusiastically during the drawing sessions. The child who confidently tackles brush and paint may need more persuasion and guidance when faced with three-dimensional construction problems.

The fact that children are inquisitive and highly impressionable has been documented over and over again. They are susceptible to sight and sound influences every waking moment of their lives, yet they are not always discriminative in their choices. Quite often the trite and tasteless in their environment make as strong an impact on them as the aesthetic, well-designed product. It is a major responsibility of the teacher to guide the child toward more artistic choices and to provide him with daily experiences to create and appreciate art. Children in school need the understanding, approbation, and guidance a sympathetic teacher provides, but they also thrive on the friendship, approval, spirited competition, and intellectual rivalry of their classmates. To grow, to mature, the child must possess a certain amount of security and self-confidence, an inquiring nature, and a stimulating, nurturing environment at home and at school.

Since no two children are alike, it is impossible to categorize them by grade or by age. A teacher encounters a wide range of behavioral characteristics in any given grade. Youngsters in school may come from different backgrounds. They may have had different experiences. Their problems and needs are not the same. Yet in order to understand them and help them grow through art, the teacher must be aware of those child characteristics that have been identified with certain age groups by researchers in educational psychology, sociology, and child study. For a more detailed, more sequential description of children's growth and behavior, the reader is referred to Appendices A and B. However, a word of caution is necessary at this point. The traits and characteristics indicated there are broad guidelines to understanding children in general and may not necessarily apply to a specific or individual child.

It is important that teachers have some understanding of the natural graphic abilities of the children in their classes in order to appreciate their developmental possibilities and limitations. The elementary art program that emphasizes quality, however, demands more of the student than what he does naturally. It is true that a small fraction of children perceive, draw, and compose sensitively with a special skill in using line, color, pattern, texture, and space, but the majority of youngsters in the elementary schools today must be guided, stimulated, and persuaded toward richer utilization of design and compositional elements, toward fuller awareness of their environment in its multiple aspects.

What do children really see? What do they respond to? What can they be invited to see, to feel, to hear, to identify with? If the teacher can bring the youngster to notice something he has never noticed before, to see with the inner eye, he will have started the child on a rewarding, endless, exciting journey of discovery. The teacher can help the child expand his horizons, his visual repertoire, by calling his attention to the thousand-and-one wonders in the world around him, such as:

The intricate pattern of a spider's web
The varied shapes caused by cracks in sidewalks, mudflats or ice floes
The subtle, pale colors in winter snow
The variety of grains in wood
The pattern of telephone wires criss-crossing a sky
The space breakup and design of a jungle gym
The muted colors of early spring farms and fields
The complex design of a honeycomb
The varieties of greens in summer foliage
The varied textures and pattern in tree bark
The shadows of tree branches against a wall or on the snow
The subtle shapes and colors of driftwood and autumn weeds
The graceful movements of a cat
The magnificent lines and tensions of bridges
The unusual cornices of historic buildings
The intriguing abstract designs of torn, deteriorated, outdoor billboards
The filigree pattern in leaves and insect wings
The variety and texture in stone walls and walks
The patterns of frost on a windowpane

The miracle of growing things
The ever-changing formations of clouds
The dew on early morning flowers and grass
The reflections in water
The moody colors of a foggy or rainy day
The flashing colors of stop lights, neon signs, beacons, and patrol cars
The rich luminosity of stained glass windows
The remarkable skeletal structure of man, animal, and plant
The subtle patina on aged metal
The patterns of contoured farms and cities from the air
The oil slick patterns on harbor waters
The organic and varied shapes of rocks and pebbles
The subtle colors of moss on rock and stone
The color orchestrations in the sky at dawn and dusk
The shimmer of harvest wheat in the wind
The fiery smoke of foundries
The tracks of animals in the snow
The rhythmic beauty of the ballet
The grace of a jet stream

The child is influenced daily by environmental factors which teachers cannot always control. Television, the press, radio, movies, the theater, musical recordings, store-window displays, magazine illustrations, paperback and record album covers, cars, clothes, and package design shape his developing taste and determine his cultural values. What a qualitative art program can do, in some measure, is to help the child be more selective, more discriminative, and more aesthetically sensitive in the many important choices he will make in his life.

3

THE TEACHER'S ROLE

A creative, enthusiastic, imaginative, adaptive, sympathetic, and constantly resourceful teacher is the essential catalyst in the development and implementation of a qualitative program in elementary art. The teacher of the art class must be an organizer, housekeeper, counselor, resource expediter, referee, adventurer, and lover of children.

Without a well-prepared and dedicated teacher at the helm, the art program may capsize in a sea of hasty, last-minute decisions, in trite and instantaneous activities, or in chaotic, pseudotherapeutic play sessions. The school that boasts a fine physical plant, a rich materials budget, and an administration sympathetic to art is fortunate, indeed, but if it does not attract teachers who are prepared to teach art confidently, creatively, developmentally, and qualitatively, then it has little chance of achieving and implementing an art program of promise and significance.

The reference to the teacher's dedication is deliberate. Dedication is, and always will be, a vital teaching asset in a democratic society. It goes beyond classroom expertise and management. Nothing is said, it is true, in the teacher's contract about dedication, not even in the small print. Nor is there anything explicit in the agreement about the requisites of love, patience, and sympathetic understanding that go hand in hand with good teaching. Unselfish dedication and enthusiastic involvement, whenever and wherever they occur, are in most instances freewill gifts of a devoted teacher and cannot be measured except perhaps in the amount of inner satisfaction and fulfillment they bring.

The best teachers of elementary art, whether classroom teacher or special art consultant, are creative, adaptive people. They work hard to understand the basic premises, techniques, and evaluative processes of the creative act; they learn how to organize mate-

The ever-renewing circle of life is all around us in exquisite and varied forms. The classroom teacher of art should turn to design in nature for constant inspiration and must learn to guide the children to notice the subtle varieties in the petals of flowers, the interstices of a spider's web, the feathers of a bird.

rials, tools, space, and time schedules to produce exemplary working conditions in classroom or art room, and they structure and implement the art program to meet the present and future needs of their students. They enrich the lives of their pupils through daily experiences in some phase of art discovery. They are constantly searching for ideas and art processes that can renew the children's interest in a project when the initial excitement wanes. In their enthusiasm, which they display unselfishly, they encourage the youngsters to open their eyes to the design, color, form, rhythm, texture, and pattern in the world around them, in both natural and manmade wonders. They identify themselves with their students. They do not always play it safe. They are excited and elated when a student makes a discovery or masters a skill. They are genuinely concerned when a student encounters a problem.

Wise teachers plan the art discussion period, the motivating question-and-answer session, or the preliminary show-and-tell segment with special care. They do not leave this important part of the art lesson to chance or last-minute inspiration. In most instances they prepare a written outline of their strategy. Because the time alloted to art in so many elementary schools is minimal, teachers must phrase their questions to elicit the richest responses in the shortest time. Their queries are usually the leading kind, seldom calling for one specific solution. They avoid blind-alley questions, positing, instead, those that open up new avenues of discovery.

16

Teachers should explore in college, and later on their own, the techniques and processes they plan to use in their classes, utilizing if possible those art materials that will be available to them in their schools. TOP—Oil pastel on black construction paper. CENTER and BOTTOM—"Found materials" collage. Teacher workshop projects.

To keep the art program a vital growing part of the curriculum, teachers of art build and keep up to date as many art resources as they can, including reproductions, photographs, color slides, film strips and loops, magazine articles and illustrations, recordings, illustrated art books, and examples of student art projects.

Teachers of art develop expertise and confidence through continuous involvement with exciting art media and techniques. They experiment with the new materials and new processes now available in order to share them with their students. They do not assign a new project to the class before exploring its possibilities and its limitations on their own. The best teachers continue to search for new variations utilizing familiar art media, new approaches to student motivation, and new evaluative strategies in order to keep their own teaching interest and skills at a high level and to enrich themselves as vital, creative people.

Discriminative teachers of art learn to see differences as well as similarities in the graphic expressions of children. They learn to build on these differences and similarities. They discover, if they are perceptive, that no two interpretations of a shared experience by the children will look exactly alike. In one instance they may find a bold, spontaneous approach; in another there may be a sensitive and delicate delineation. One child may be concerned with the intricate designs of pattern and texture, another youngster may reveal an imaginative and sparkling sense of color.

More projects from teachers' workshops. TOP—Colored tissue collage over ink sketch on white construction paper. CENTER—Lino print over colored tissue background. BOTTOM—Lino print over colored magazine ad.

17

A positive, cheerful, animated, and outgoing personality is a major asset for teachers of art. They should try to develop a genuine interest in what the children are creating and discovering; they must learn to be patient, calm, and adaptable. Children want to believe in their teacher. They need the security of a teacher's confidence in the subject being taught. Youngsters come to rely on their teachers for help with important decisions, with possible solutions to perplexing problems. They are skeptical of the teacher who confuses them with vague generalizations, who places all the responsibility in their hands.

Teachers of art learn to listen to the child's description of his experiences, both real and imaginary, with genuine interest. They avoid a casual, noncommital approach. Instead, their excitement for the project-in-process is evident in their action, their words, their eyes.

Teachers of art learn to cultivate a ready sense of humor. It saves many a disastrous situation. Teachers who really *care* about children avoid talking down to them and most important of all do not underestimate the capabilities of any child of any age or the child's capacity to explore and to discover the wonderful horizons of art—its freedoms, its disciplines, and its rewards.

One result of the current confusion over objectives and goals in art education today is the false front so many teachers of art are almost forced to erect in order to please all parties concerned. In too many instances, we find art teachers apologizing for making

Some art techniques, such as the tempera batik by a teacher illustrated at left, may require more time for materials preparation and clean-up but upper-grade children often find them exciting and challenging.

suggestions to children, for initiating projects, for teaching art fundamentals and techniques. In order to win the approbation of the behaviorists, such statements as "the children decided," "someone in the class mentioned," "the students made their own plans" are commonly used in articles describing classroom art projects. Let's be honest and clear the air, once and for all. Where exciting, colorful, and dynamic elementary art programs and practices exist, the classroom teacher of art, or the special art teacher, is on the job—guiding, challenging, directing, stimulating, questioning, suggesting, approving, prompting, planning, coaching, advising, and organizing. In other words, *teaching!*

The initial strategies in teaching an art lesson are very crucial to its ultimate success. Projects initiated with adequate planning, with preliminary experimentation in the particular material or technique involved, and with exciting motivational resources on hand add immeasurably to the substance and continuity of the art program. Experienced and perceptive teachers are quite often able to envisage the entire project or process with all its accompanying problems. This does not imply that they are not alert to innovative unscheduled developments that may occur during the project. It does mean that they are continually aware of the broad and encompassing objectives of the lesson.

Another vital element in the planning of every art project is the housekeeping involved. The teacher must organize classroom facilities so that there will be adequate working space, a sufficient supply of materials and tools, adequate storage facilities for projects-in-process and for those completed, effective clean-up equipment and procedures, plus easily accessible supply and demonstration stations.

Budgeting the time allotted to the art lesson is a very important factor. The children should not feel that they are being rushed through any phase of the project. Wise teachers carefully plan the amount of time needed for preliminary discussion and dialogue, for demonstrations and motivational presentations, for distribution and collection of materials and tools, and for classroom clean-up.

Teachers of art will find that both they and their students can profit if they use the chalkboard to outline the specific objectives or criteria for the project undertaken. In this manner the varied goals or possibilities are much more easily identified, and evaluations for the completed products can be more clearly defined. In the upper grades especially, these evaluative criteria written on chalkboard or bulletin board augment the teacher's effectiveness and are a ready checklist for the children, affording them the opportunity to make their own evaluations of work in process, thus minimizing their dependence on the teacher and discouraging the "Am I finished?" refrain.

Children in the primary grades who have difficulty in reading chalkboard instructions will benefit more by having the teacher simply discuss the objectives of the project with them, giving individual suggestions from time to time as they work.

Another vital requisite for a qualitative elementary art program is an atmosphere or climate conducive to the development of individual expression. Wise teachers allow the child to work independently until they see that the youngster is in need of further motivational fuel, then provide him with rich incentives to reach new levels of artistic growth.

A teacher's success in art class is often based on the empathic rapport which must develop between instructor and students. The desired relationship may take a while to develop but once the teacher establishes a climate of cooperation and of mutual understanding, this gift to guide and challenge the youngster becomes the critical point of teaching efficiency.

One of the most frequent questions asked by university and college students preparing to be teachers and echoed by teachers already in the field is "Just how much help should the teacher of art give a child?" Some answers may be found in the following description of an art project taught by four second-grade teachers, each opting a different approach.

Teacher A

A second grade class is engaged in drawing a picture of a live cat and kittens brought to school by one of the children. Their teacher suggests that the youngsters look carefully at the cat and kittens, which are placed on a desk or table in the front of the class, before they begin coloring with their crayons on white or manila paper. Whatever the children draw is accepted without question or evaluative comment. The working time allotted is approximately 30 to 45 minutes. Children who finish early are instructed to put their pictures on the teacher's desk and are assigned other studies.

Teacher B

Teacher B carries this project a step further. Before the preliminary drawing begins, this instructor monitors a discussion session dealing with the cat and kittens, their size relationships, their predominant characteristics, their movements, their color, their texture, their special cat qualities and aspects. Composition and design, as such, are not discussed and, as in the case of the first teacher, no further help or art criticism is offered once the children begin crayoning. Because more time is given to the actual motivation, the time allotment is increased to two periods of 45 minutes—one to complete the basic sketch and the other to finish the coloring.

Teacher C

Teacher C with a broader preparation in art, with a background of university or college classes where actual art techniques were introduced, moves in a richer direction by introducing the children to the possibilities of design, composition, and technique. As in the case of the second teacher, a motivational session is held after which *art* considerations enter

the picture. Colored construction paper is suggested as a more exciting background for the drawings. Children are allowed to choose the color they wish from a large assortment. The teacher recommends that the children draw their cat and kittens large so others in class will be able to see them, to fill the space of the paper. A preliminary sketch in white chalk or very light crayon is suggested so that children can plan their composition. The teacher advises the children that the crayon colors may be tried out first on the reverse side of their paper to discover new possibilities. Suggestions for achieving richness of colors are made. Pressing hard with the crayon is emphasized. Attention is called to dark and light colors, to color contrast, to pattern and texture. Following this discussion, which includes the reaction to and an awareness of the cat and kittens, plus the introduction of enriching art factors, the active role of the teacher ends and the youngsters are on their own during the picture making. Time allotment is approximately 1 hour for the motivation session, including the sketch. The coloring of the picture usually takes two 45-minute sessions.

Teacher D

Teacher D is an exemplary teacher who enjoys teaching art in its varied aspects to children and is prepared to make every minute of the limited art period rich and rewarding for the youngsters in class.

Crayon drawings on 12"x18" assorted colored construction paper. Grade 2. The teacher's cat and kittens were the frisky models. Preliminary drawings in light crayon were made during the first 50 minute session. Crayoning richly took two more 50-minute periods.

21

Teacher D, like Teacher C, plans and expedites an exciting, motivational session dealing with the children's immediate responses to the cat and kittens, with the many ways that art language and art structure can help the youngsters express themselves more successfully in visual terms. This teacher employs the elements and principles of art with their basic vocabulary of line, shape, form, value, color, pattern, texture, repetition, balance, contrast, and emphasis to give substance and purpose to the child's expressive act.

It is what Teacher D does once the children begin working on their drawings and paintings that makes this teacher unique. Encouraging each youngster to make his picture a personal statement, Teacher D watches for the child who may need special help in getting started on his drawing or coloring. At the beginning of the picture-making, this teacher wisely remains in the background yet is always ready to handle specific problems as they arise. As the creative excitement of the children grows, as the compositions develop, this teacher identifies enthusiastically with each student's discoveries, sharing them with the class.

Tempera paint in its varied flowing colors is still one of the most popular art mediums universally enjoyed by children. The paintings on this and facing page are by first-grade youngsters. Size 24" x 36".

The special quality that distinguishes high-caliber teachers of art from the average instructor is their ability to respond intelligently, sympathetically, and purposefully to the child's creative, artistic efforts, to talk to the child knowledgeably, sincerely, and honestly about his art work, to evaluate it, giving it importance and significance in the child's eyes by paying serious attention to it.

Four teachers; four strategies. The most creative and most qualitative approach takes a little more time, a little more preparation, a little more concern for the efforts of every student. Yet, teachers should realize that in many instances young students do not appreciate or enjoy a new art process or media until they become deeply involved in it. Once the youngsters see the possibilities in a technique or art material, their interest grows. This is why teachers must plan the introductory session of any new or difficult art project with care. If the art technique is strange to the children, the teacher should enlist the aid of the students in demonstrating the basic procedures, presenting the technical information in easily assimilated segments. Difficult steps should be repeated if necessary.

23

In a complex technique, it is advisable to have students explore or experiment with the specific materials or tools of the project before they engage in the final work. The teacher, too, should know what tools and techniques are best in order to guide the student in the process. Innovation and exploration of art media by the students should always be encouraged.

For the very young children simple procedures and techniques should be clearly explained. In the case of a multicrayon project, for example, the teacher would need to describe and emphasize the kind of crayon pressure to be exerted and clarify the possibilities of the color sequence in order to help the youngsters achieve a reasonable success.

The subject, content, or theme and its adaptability to the selected technique must be taken into consideration by the teacher. It might prove frustrating for a student to make a preliminary sketch in fine pencil lines and then lose this detailed interpretation in the bold and heavy strokes of a chalk or tempera painting.

The teacher must be ready to help the child relate his preliminary sketch or drawing to the final technique. For example, the utilization of brush and ink or a felt-nib marker as the initial sketching tool for a linoleum print composition is recommended because both brush and ink and the blunt felt-nib relate to the strong lines produced by a linoleum gouge.

The teacher is the necessary catalyst and bridge builder in the art class. It is the teacher's responsibility to help build a climate in which purposeful endeavor, search and inquiry, individuality, and creativity thrive. When teachers of art are truly concerned about the expressive growth of the children in their classes, they plan and do things the youngsters may not always approve. They may ask their students to set higher standards of performance for themselves. They may demand a little more effort than the children have been accustomed to making. They could take the easy way out by letting the youngsters do what they please in art but, being concerned and conscientious, they continue to set the highest creative challenges for their students.

ABOVE—No two children draw a tree in exactly the same way. College students preparing to teach art explore various techniques and develop confidence to guide children creatively. Illustrations on opposite page from the art education classes of author Frank Wachowiak. Left to right beginning at top: oil pastel resist, plaster relief, tempera batik, oil pastel, collage, crayon engraving, crayon resist, container construction, vegetable print.

4

AVENUES TO MOTIVATION

Teachers everywhere agree that most children need some form of motivation, visual or otherwise, to achieve the highest potential in their art. In almost every elementary art guide published, repeated reference is made to the fact that a child must have something to say before he can express it in visual form.

Inspiration for a youngster's art expression may come from many sources. It may spring from his experiences at school, home, or church, from his playground activities, from visits to museums, art galleries, fairs, zoos, gardens, national parks, shopping centers, circuses, parades, animal shows, races, sports, and games, from movies, television, theater, radio, books, comics, magazines, and musical recordings. The responsibility, however, for reactivating these motivational experiences and giving them a significance and an immediacy to trigger the youngster into an art expression is primarily the teacher's.

Teachers must be prepared to enrich the child's store of knowledge, to tap his recall powers. Specifically they might ask the youngster the leading questions: *How? What? Why? Where? When?* concerning an event or an experience. This avenue of questioning should be designed to encourage the child's seeing and perceiving, not just his verbal responding. The important consideration here is the development of an awareness and a visual discrimination. The teacher must be ready to help the child clarify and emphasize the significant aspects of the experience.

In many instances the teacher will find it necessary to provide the child with motivating material through planned field trips and varied vicarious experiences in the classroom itself. That is why teachers must have on hand or at close call a rich fund of audiovisual resources such as color slides, filmstrips, art

Inspiration for children's art is as near as the school yard. Teachers should take advantage of the immediate environment for subject matter inspiration. Here very young children use 18" x 24" lightweight cardboard as sketching pads for their preliminary drawings from nature.

films, examples of student work in several techniques, color reproductions of paintings by established artists, musical recordings, and artifacts of all kinds.

The most vital art project motivations are based on vivid and meaningful personal experiences. Nothing replaces the actually perceived object or a direct contact for intense, immediate stimulation. Sketching trips to a farm, fire station, dairy, greenhouse, factory, or building site are recommended. Guest visits to the class by an athlete, a serviceman, an astronaut, a musician, or a dancer may sometimes be arranged to enrich the student's store of ideas. Live animals, birds, or pets brought to school will evoke stimulating and enthusiastic responses from the children that can trigger colorful art expression.

In the classroom or art room itself, the teacher can display nature's varied forms of fruit, vegetables, sea shells, seaweed, coral, driftwood, bark, mounted collections of insects, butterflies, rocks, gourds, minerals, live and dried plants, mounted birds, and animals or live fish in an aquarium. Still-life objects such as flowers, bottles, lanterns, clocks, musical instruments, lamps, and a variety of antique Americana can become the inspiration for many drawing and painting projects especially in the upper grades.

At every opportunity teachers should tactfully discourage the student's dependency on, or utilization of, visual stereotypes, clichés or conventional shorthand symbols. They should minimize the "draw what you want" or "what I did on my vacation" assignments by emphasizing more drawing experiences based on things which can be immediately observed, touched, studied, explored, and felt.

Teachers should help the child respond to nature and its wonders in more than one way. They might call his attention, for example, to a butterfly in a pragmative, objective way by describing it as "a tiger swallowtail belonging to the Lepidoptera family." They should, however, bring him to see its design and structure as well, asking the child to use his artist's eye to see the insect's linear qualities, the variety of colors, the pattern and textures, the butterfly's unique shape. This dual interpretation and description of nature in her myriad aspects should be encouraged in every art experience where environmental forms are the source of the child's expression.

The materials, tools, and techniques of the various art projects can become motivating devices, too, and, in many instances, may be the special catalyst that fires the student's efforts. In the primary grades the introduction of the new, vibrant pigments and colors in oil pastel, poster paint, crayon, and papers brings added excitement to coloring and painting. The free-flowing felt or nylon markers in assorted colors elicit an enthusiastic response from the youngsters in all grades. Tissue paper in a host of colors delights the upper-grade child who can handle it confidently as he discovers new colors through tearing and overlapping tissue over tissue.

In the upper grades, too, the teacher can whet the creative appetites of the youngsters by introducing them to the very new *day-glo* and psychedelic poster paints, to melted crayon for encaustic painting, to scrap vinyls and glass for mosaics, to waxes and dyes for batiks, to plaster for carving and bas reliefs, to metals for casting, to glazes for ceramics, and to scrap wire, plastic, wood, and boxes for construction.

In recent years, critics of art education have called attention to the proliferation of new media and techniques in the school art programs and its deleterious effects. Though some of the criticism is justifiable, it is not the new materials themselves that are the source of the problem, but the manner in which some teachers and students use them that is suspect. It is a generally known fact that a student with the newest, finest pigments and tools may produce an ugly, horrible work, whereas another student utilizing only discarded scraps from an attic, alley, or junk heap may create an object of singular beauty. The fault, to paraphrase a great writer, lies not in the materials themselves but in the expressive sensibilities of the creator.

The introductory segment of an art lesson or project should spark the interest of the youngsters as much as possible. It is unfair to expect students to be challenged or excited by a series of art assignments or experiences that begin simply with the teacher saying, "Draw what you want today," or "Paint the way you feel." The teacher of the art class should devote as much time to the presentation of an art project as is given to the preparation of a math or science unit.

There are many effective ways to begin an art lesson. These include showing a film, filmstrip, or color slides on the project theme; viewing slides or examples of previous work; guiding the class in a discussion on related experiences; conducting a field trip to enrich the students knowledge of the subject matter; playing musical recordings or tapes to create the mood of the particular visual theme chosen; demonstrating the technical process with student participation; calling attention to a bulletin display prepared for the art project; introducing a special guest who might talk, perform, or model for the students; using selected poems, songs, drama, or fiction as project or subject matter stimulation.

With this varied arsenal of motivational procedures planned well in advance, the student can look forward to the art class as a unique and rewarding period of the school day. Each project, each technique, each age group demands its own pattern of motivation, and only the teacher with a rich repertoire of ideas will be able to bring to the art program or art lesson, the special ingredients that give it significance.

One of the most common problems the teacher of an art class faces is the lagging of student interest after the initial excitement of a new project or technique has dissipated. This is especially true in those situations where the youngsters do not set high enough standards for themselves and are satisfied with only a superficial effort, or for those who have not developed a real concern for, or identification with, the subject matter involved.

There are always a number of children in an art class who complete their work sooner than the others, who feel they have exhausted the possibilities of the project while their classmates are still busily involved in their creations. This situation presents a real problem, because it involves an interpretation of the fine balance between what the child can honestly accomplish in art with sensitive guidance and what he is often willing to settle for. If at the outset of the project, the teacher, in collaboration with the students, sets up general goals and criteria of achievement in technique, composition, structure, and design, then the recurring problem of the child who rushes through his work will not be such a critical one.

These criteria, like a check list, could be posted on chalkboard or bulletin board for student reference as they work. Such a procedure could also alleviate one of the major quandaries facing the teacher, that is, being able to guide each of the thirty or more students effectively and still manage the multiple responsibilities of classroom management. When questions pertaining to the project arise, the teacher could clarify them with the entire class by pointing to specific objectives on the board, rather than wasting time by repeating them to each student individually. Quite often work in progress by youngsters can be shown to the class with appropriate constructive criticism to emphasize the goals of the particular technique or project and to call attention to possible variations in expression. A suggestion given to one student will often trigger new ideas and possibilities for other students in class who may have reached a creative impasse or plateau.

At the upper-grade level the practice of writing brief constructive remarks on the back of the student's work, or on slips of paper attached to the youngster's projects, has proven beneficial in many instances and in a number of ways. It gives the teacher a chance to evaluate the class work at a time free of distractions and other responsibilities; it insures the possibility that every student will receive specific, individual help at some time during the project; it provides the youngster with a definite, working direction for each part of the next art period that keeps him purposefully occupied while the teacher attends to routine tasks and special problems. This strategy for project evaluation, though time-consuming, can help the busy teacher implement individualized instruction, giving purpose and significance to the art program.

Another popular and successful method of renewing student interest in their art is to praise their creations and efforts which exhibit and illustrate dynamic composition, sensitive line, unique texture and pattern, unusual space delineation, personal style, and vibrant color orchestration.

Interesting objects to trigger drawing experiences can be found all around us. The ordinary can become extraordinary through the eyes of the child artist. The teacher should enlist the children's aid in scouting for exciting visual treasures to share and exhibit in the classroom to make it a perpetually stimulating place.

Because children can absorb or retain only a few ideas at one time, the teacher should not overwhelm them with an avalanche of suggestions. Motivation should be provided in small doses, introducing, if possible, a new and exciting attention-getter each time the art class meets. The following motivational resources are suggested as tried-and-tested possibilities:

Reproduction of paintings, sculpture, prints, and crafts that can supplement and intensify the objectives of the project.

Photographs in color or black and white that can extend the student's visual store of experiences.

Color slides of paintings, drawings, sculpture, prints, architecture, sculpture crafts, design in nature and man-made objects, creative work by other children, work illustrating technical stages of a project, shots of people in action, in sports, in costume, animals, birds, fish, and insects.

Filmstrips and cartridge tapes on art techniques, art history, and on correlated subject matter such as biology, anthropology, botany, ecology, geology, geography, travel, space exploration and technology.

Films, TV films, and tapes that apply to a particular theme undertaken.

Books (stories, plays, poems, biographies), periodicals, and pamphlets that can broaden the knowledge of both student and teacher and help bring a richer interpretation of the subject chosen.

Recordings (disc or tape) of music of dramatizations and poetry, of sounds of various geographic regions, of city and country sounds, of nature's forces, of machines, ships, trains, rockets, of circuses, and fairs.

Guest speakers, performers, and models such as astronauts, clowns, dancers, actors, scuba divers, pilots, athletes, singing groups, and musicians.

Resource and sketching trips to science and historical museums, art museums and galleries, artists' studios, farms, factories, wharves, airports, observatories, bus and railroad terminals, bridge sites, national parks, zoos, shopping centers, historical monuments, boat marinas. (Be sure trips are planned in advance. Make a survey of the sketching site beforehand, if possible, to check on any hazards. Clear permission with the school principal early so that necessary travel arrangements can be made.)

Models for art class observation and drawing can include live or mounted mammals, birds, fish, flowers, and plant life, dried fall weeds, beehives, bird nests, insect or butterfly collections, fish in aquariums, terrariums, ant colonies, pets, skulls, rocks and pebbles, seaweed and seashells, also assorted still-life material—fruit, vegetables, lanterns, kettles, vases, clocks, teapots, bottles, fish net, burlap, bold patterned cloth remnants, and old lamps.

Artifacts from other cultures, other countries, such as masks, carvings, containers, textiles, ceramics, toys, tools, icons, fetishes, dolls, puppets, and armor.

Examples of children's art work in varied media.

Demonstrations of art techniques by the teachers and students.

Constructive critiques by the students of art work in process with the positive guidance of the teacher.

Introduction of a new material or tool, or a new use for common materials, or familiar tools.

Planned exhibits and bulletin-board displays that relate to the art project.

OPPOSITE PAGE—A changing exhibit of artifacts and crafts can help expand the children's cultural awareness and often serves as the special catalyst for their own creative and aesthetic growth.

Introduction of an art design element or principle or a special emphasis on some compositional element, such as value, texture, or color relationship.

Assorted objects and equipment to help expand the student's visual horizons, such as microscopes, prisms, kaleidoscopes, color-faceted eye-glasses, *touch-me* kinetics, color machines, liquid light lamps, telescopes, microscopic projectors, and black light.

Strategic timing is of the utmost importance in successful motivation. The teacher must be able to sense when the children have reached a dead-end and need stronger incentives to insure progress in their work. The beginning of the class period is usually the best time to introduce new motivations, new materials, and new processes because the youngsters are most receptive then. The teacher should not interrupt a class busily engaged in their work to present a point that could have been made at the outset of the lesson. Time allotments for motivational sessions should be wisely budgeted so that the children will not feel cheated out of their studio or activity period. The perceptive teacher learns through experience to gauge the listening alertness, the attention or interest span of the students, and plans the whole sequence of motivation, discussion, demonstration, studio, and evaluation realistically and purposefully.

34

TOP—A colorful example of San Blas Island Indian molas. CENTER—Southeast American Indian Kachina dolls and Navaho rug. BOTTOM—Hand crafted rag dolls exhibited at the Plum Nelly Mountain Festival in Georgia.

SOME MOTIVATIONAL RESOURCES

Teachers will find many occasions during the school year to use the following motivational resources and thereby enrich the art program.

Mounted birds, fish, animals
Acetate, celluloid, or plexiglass sheets in various colors
New *day-glo* colors and papers
An aquarium of colorful, tropical fish
Ant farm or bee colony
Bells from the Far East
Duck decoys
Eskimo sculpture in soapstone or whalebone
Fish netting
Indian corn, hedge apples
Gourds, squash
Indian Kachina or Japanese Kokeshi dolls
Magnifying glass
Window display mannequins
Masks: African, Mexican, Japanese Nō or Bugaku,
      Clown, Mardi Gras, Indian
Mexican, Indian pottery
Butterfly collections
Model cars and engines
Musical instruments
Navaho Indian rugs
Old-fashioned hats
Lanterns, clocks, old lamps
Bird cages and birds
Theatrical costumes and face make-up
Texture table
Puppets from various countries
Santos figures from Mexico and the Phillipines
Colored tissue paper

Spotlights
Full-length mirror
Japanese paper fish-kites
Glass fishing floats
Bicycles, motorcycles, helmets
Sports equipment
Multicolored containers
Assorted bottles
Stained glass
Cloth remnants
Wall paper sample books
Antique Americana
Contemporary posters, travel posters

36

5
CONTINUITY IN ART

In no other subject area in the elementary school is continuity of learning so misunderstood and so poorly implemented as it is in art. Most classroom teachers are aware of sequential growth in elementary math, science, and language and of the specific content and skills to be mastered by the children at each succeeding level. They can usually help the child build with confidence on the previous year's learnings in these areas.

In elementary art, however, this is seldom the case. Teachers of the upper grades are often in the dark concerning the art program in the primary grades if, in fact, such a program exists. In too many schools art projects are a hodge-podge of spur-of-the-moment activities unrelated to each other or to the child's earlier art experiences. Too often these art lessons are hastily concocted to fit in, but not to run over, the 30 minute period per week allotted to art.

Because there is very little planning when dealing with sequential art learnings, children from grades 1 through 6 are often fed a monotonous diet of endless crayon pictures, usually seat-work assignments, to illustrate the various aspects of social studies or literature. It is natural for the youngsters to become disinterested and bored when they feel they are not growing in new art skills and techniques. Parents, too, are questioning the validity of art activities that are little more than play periods.

The following outline of a sequential, developmental program in elementary art, describing the implementation of simple to complex art concepts, is the culmination of many rewarding years of teaching and researching art at the elementary school level and of countless seminars involving hundreds of classroom teachers, art teachers, art consultants, and college art educators. It should prove of significant value to those elementary classroom teachers who need specific help in the important task of planning their art program and in the critical area of art process and product evaluation.

The young child expresses himself in an almost inimitable way. The teacher can gently lead him to notice the many aspects of nature's beauty around him, can help him with special art techniques when the need arises, but what he depicts so honestly, so naively, so boldly is colored by a mystique that often defies explanation. Note how economically and directly he makes his statement about flowers, spiderwebs, and insects in the crayon engraving on the opposite page. Grade 3, Danielsville, Georgia. In circle above a youngster applies a rich layer of crayon for his engraving.

GRADES ONE AND TWO

Encourage the children to make drawings based on personal experiences and observations but reward the imaginative, make-believe approaches as well. Provide many opportunities for them to draw from real things, including plants in and around the school, animal pets brought to class, insect collections, flower arrangements, their classmates as models, sports equipment, games, and the many visual inspirations gained from field trips.

Suggest that they draw fairly large so that they can introduce the details they consider important. Encourage them to fill the space of their compositions or paper. In most instances, the more visual images or ideas they include in their compositions, the more exciting and interrelated their drawings become.

Specific challenges such as "think as you draw," "do not rush through your drawing," and "draw the big, important things first" may be suggested at this stage. The following rhyme provides clues the youngsters can use to evaluate their compositions.

> Something big, something small
> Something short, something tall
> Something dark, something light
> Helps to make your drawing right!

Encourage the children to see the possibilities of the drawn line, the different kinds of lines, including the different tools that make lines, including crayon, chalk, pastel, pencil, pen, a stick in sand, a finger in wet paint.

Experiences in design and pattern-making should be part of every child's drawing repertoire. Promote discovery and exploitation of varied patterns, stripes, plaids, dots, and circles, scribbles and jig-saw or zig-zag designs. Encourage discovery of pattern in the clothes people wear, in the furnishings of the school and of the home, in packaging and posters, and in the wonders of nature.

Suggested drawing themes: *Fun in the Snow and on the Playground, Picking Flowers in the Garden, Me and My Pet, Playing Ball, Skipping Rope, On the Jungle Gym, The Merry-go-Round, A Rabbit's or Gopher's Home, The House Where I Live, On the Way to School, Our Community Helpers, Bugs and Beetles, Fish in the Sea, Animals in the Zoo, Noah's Ark, On the Farm, Birds in a Tree, The Circus Parade, Chicken Hatchery, The Dog Show.*

OPPOSITE PAGE. TOP—*Youngsters visited a farm and created their impressions in crayon on colored construction paper. Grade 1, Ann Arbor, Michigan.* CENTER—*A child's interpretation of a rabbit's home. Imagination and knowledge are happily wed in this crayon picture. Grade 2, Oshkosh, Wisconsin.* BOTTOM—*The rich colors of oil pastel helped his first grader say "This is my house!". Athens, Georgia.*

Introduce drawing experiences that help children appreciate their community helpers: the truck driver, lifeguard, meter maid, librarian, grocer, pharmacist, auto mechanic, doorman, garbage collector, secretary, barber, dentist, lawyer, postman, beautician, chef, TV announcer, clerk, baker, doctor, policeman, teacher, carpenter, train engineer, pilot, astronaut, waiter, milkman, farmer, stewardess, fireman, judge, bus driver, forest ranger, soldier, nurse, telephone operator, highway patrolman, janitor.

GRADES THREE AND FOUR

Continue to provide the youngsters with immediate, visually exciting material for drawing. On sketching trips scout for the unusual, the pictorially stimulating vista. Avoid the unrelieved expanse of an ocean or river, field or plain. Choose landscapes or cityscapes with multishaped structures and complex break-up of space.

Children are now more responsive to suggestions dealing with compositional structure, such as, overlapping objects and shapes to create design and space; achieving distance through relative sizes, proportions, and placements of objects on the page; creating pattern and texture through linear techniques; and drawing the line in a more controlled way to achieve variety and emphasis.

Build on the students' repertoire of drawing skills. Review the discoveries they have made concerning the potential of line. Introduce new techniques in producing line—stick and ink, brush and watercolor calligraphy, cardboard edge drawing, and the engraved line through crayon.

When children reach the fourth grade, they can be introduced to simple contour-drawing techniques. For the visual stimulus, begin with simple, uncompli-cated objects: a tennis shoe, an old leather glove, a bottle, a baseball mitt, a teapot, a football or space helmet, a fruit or vegetable. When the students' confidence increases, try a combined arrangement with one object overlapping another. Explain and demonstrate the contour method of drawing so that it is fairly clear to the children. It is very important that the child is guided to look carefully and intently at the thing or object he is drawing and that he draw very slowly. Some teachers suggest that the youngster who is using pencil in his contour line drawing press very hard as he draws. Erasures should be discouraged; instead, a second line may be drawn. The child may stop at critical or puzzling junctures, reposition his drawing tool, and continue drawing.

At this intermediate level the children can begin to use lines and juxtaposition of lines to express mood, feeling, or action.

Design knowledge and appreciation may be expanded through class discussion on the many design principles found in nature and everyday objects. Direct the youngsters' attention once more to variety of line, shape, and texture, to pattern, balance, repetition, radiation, emphasis.

The experiences of the youngsters, real or imagined, are the elemental stuff that child art is made of, but it is also true that the child who notices more, senses more, and remembers more endows his graphic images with richer content as illustrated in the opaque watercolor painting on opposite page. A Visit to the Doctor. Grade 3, Osaka, Japan.

Ask the children to bring to class various examples of natural forms such as leaves, twigs, weeds, rocks, stones, honeycombs, birds' nests, nuts, pods, sea shells, and pine cones. Capitalize on these to trigger interest in line drawings and designs.

Suggested themes for drawing: *Spring Cleaning, Washing the Car, Traffic Jam, Boarding the School Bus, On the Bus, At the Airport, At the Gas Station,* *Window Shopping, On the Train, A View from a Plane, Rare Birds, Things on a Table, Bicycle Race, Kite Festival, Tug of War, Soap-Box Derby, A Tree House, Self-Portrait or Portrait of a Friend (with sports equipment or musical instrument or family pet), A Windy Day, Fun at the Swimming Pool, The Fair, Space Ships, Undersea Station, At the Dentist's, At the Barbershop.*

41

GRADES FIVE AND SIX

Whenever possible take the youngsters on sketching field trips. Scout and select interesting sites to draw: building developments, harbors, bridges, airports, gas stations, zoos, natural museums, shopping malls, a view down a street, industrial complexes, a cluster of farm buildings.

In the upper grades, children can be guided to create interest and movement in their linear compositions by varying the placement of images or elements on the page. For example, figures, objects, or buildings might start on different levels and terminate at different levels. Objects and shapes could also be juxtaposed or overlapped to create compositional unity, direction, and shallow space.

Challenge the youngsters to become aware of the possibilities in positive and negative shapes and spaces in their compositions. Usually the more varied the objects are in size and shape (the positive elements) the more exciting the background (the negative element) becomes.

Continue implementation of expressive drawing techniques including contour and gesture approaches. The majority of the youngsters should now be able to grasp the contour drawing approach.

At this stage some of the children will attempt to achieve value through shading, stippling, or cross-hatching in their drawings. They will need guidance in the interpretation of light and dark values, of cast shadows and reflections.

Now the maturing youngster can begin to see the importance and effectiveness of incomplete objects, figures, and buildings that terminate at the edge or border of the paper creating linear avenues into the composition, lines that lead the observer into the picture. Usually the more avenues provided into the composition, the more opportunities the child has to use a variety of colors or values in the resulting shapes.

Unless the child specifically requests help, it is wiser not to introduce perspective rules or foreshortening techniques at this time. However, youngsters will now want their pictures to "look right" and will often need assistance in making their fences stand straight, sidewalks lie flat, and roads disappear in the distance. They strive for the right proportion in their figures; yet somehow the teacher must try to convince the student that making something "realistically" right does not always make it "artistically" right. They should be aware that artists have often

broken all the rules of perspective and proportion and yet have produced works of great impact and beauty.

To expand the youngster's knowledge and appreciation of master drawings, the teacher should introduce them to reproductions or books of drawings by Albrecht Dürer, Rembrandt van Rijn, Eugene Delacroix, Hokusai, Paul Klee, Edgar Degas, Pablo Picasso, Vincent van Gogh, Henri Matisse, Ben Shahn, and Andrew Wyeth. Refer them, also, to the cave drawings of Altamira and Font du Gaume, to the strong linear expressions of African and Australian aborigines as well as to the evocative drawings of the Indian and Eskimo.

Suggested drawing themes: *Figure Drawings from the Model, Space Platforms, Cities in Outer Space, Self-Portraits, Landscapes, Cityscapes, Seascapes, Rock Festival, Bicycles, Machines, Motorcycles, Dune Buggies, Horse Show, 4-H Fair, The Shopping Mall.*

The contour-line technique is perhaps the most successful drawing approach for the upper-grade child. Suggest that the youngster draw in pencil slowly, deliberately, and most important of all, look intently at what he is drawing. The illustration above is a sensitive on-the-spot study of classmates by a sixth grader in Osaka, Japan. Note how every hair is delineated, how every line defines an important contour.

GRADES ONE AND TWO

Begin teaching color awareness with the everyday crayons and paints the child uses in class. Identify the primary colors red, yellow, blue and the secondary colors orange, green, purple. Check records of children for evidences of color blindness.

Encourage the child to create rich hues with his crayons by pressing harder as he colors his pictures. Demonstrate what is possible with a strong pressure on the crayon.

Introduce the youngsters to the exciting world of color through the media of varicolored tissue paper, colored cellophane, or plexiglass. Have the children overlap these colored elements against a window light or on a sheet of white paper. Ask them to identify the new colors they create by overlapping and mingling colors.

Invite the children to bring to class, to share and identify, nature's varied store of colors in leaves, flowers, twigs, pebbles, stones, rocks, bark, pine cones, sea shells, seed pods, and nuts. Challenge them to see the variety of greens in leaves, the many hues in the bark of a tree.

Call the children's attention to the myriad of colors in their immediate surroundings—in their clothes, their books, the paintings on display in the school. Help them to identify the bright, warm, sunny colors such as yellow, orange, pink, red, gold and the happy events associated with them—the circus, the fair, summer fun. Include, too, in your presentation the dark, deep colors of blue, purple, green, turquoise and the images they invoke—the mysterious night, the ocean deep, the forest dark, the worlds of outer space.

Take advantage of the many stimulating games, toys, and color constructions, commercially available, to build color awareness—the prism, color wheel, and kaleidoscope.

Encourage color matching using *found materials* and colored scraps of art paper. Have a box for each range of colors—blues of all tints and shades in one box, greens in another, and so forth. Hold a matching color game.

Develop awareness through color mingling by letting primary colors flow together on white drawing paper, blowing colored inks or watercolors together on white paper, or dropping colors in a fold of white paper and blotting.

OPPOSITE PAGE. TOP—Segments of broken stained glass glued to a discarded pane of clear glass. Preliminary design painted in black enamel on reverse side of glass. Grade 2, Oshkosh, Wisconsin. CENTER—Handcrafted gift balls in colored silk cord from Japan afford exciting visual stimulation. BOTTOM—Color is all around us. County and state fair concessions often shock the visitor with a riot of primary colors.

GRADES THREE AND FOUR

Review color learnings from grades 1 and 2. Involve the children in projects that call for many color choices, for example, collage (cut and paste) utilizing varicolored construction or tissue paper or fabric remnants; printing with *found objects* on colored construction paper; creating crayon or oil pastel resist paintings; making mobiles or mosaics with colored pieces of glass; melting crayon shavings between two sheets of wax paper; creating a color environment in one corner of the classroom utilizing *found objects,* crepe paper, balloons, hula hoops, posters, and so forth.

Encourage the youngsters now to experiment with an expanded range of colors plus their tints and shades. Discuss the implications of warm and cool colors. Encourage projects that involve the exploitation of related colors to capture a theme or mood. Many youngsters are now mature enough to tackle the intricacies of color neutralization, to appreciate the subtle contrast of dull colors against bright colors. In watercolor and opaque (tempera) painting projects, the children can be guided to mix new colors for a particular mood—the browns, the many shades of green and blue, the grays, and the flesh tones.

Invite the children to discover complex color orchestrations through projects such as fadeless colored paper weaving; multicrayon designs that begin with scribble, jigsaw, or patchwork-quilt break-up of space; mosaics utilizing magazine-ad and book-cover colors for tesserae.

GRADES FIVE AND SIX

Review color knowledge and color discoveries made in previous grades. Recapitulate primary, secondary, intermediate colors, the color wheel, complementary and related colors, color values, the tints and shades, color intensities, the neutralization or dulling of colors, the way color affects people, the colors of the advertising media, the colors of ceremonials, customs, and rituals, and the symbolic meanings of colors in different cultures.

Use mood music as a background for free, expressive painting. Let the music influence the children's selection of colors.

Whenever possible take the youngsters to exhibits featuring the new color and light shows, the exciting black-light displays.

Challenge the children to construct or create a color "environment" or "happening" with *found color materials* such as discarded ribbons, wrapping paper, colored tissue, cellophane, yarn, balloons, beach balls, beach towels, hula hoops, crepe paper in sheets and streamers, paper flowers, colored boxes, posters, party decorations, colorful wrapping papers, and cloth or fabric remnants in the boldest, brightest patterns available.

Continue building color awareness by directing the attention of the youngsters to color exploitation in their everyday world—to billboards, posters, magazine covers and ads, packaging, clothing, cosmetics, lighting fixtures, interior decoration, foods, book jackets, record albums, and new cars.

Augment the students' color knowledge and appreciation by scheduling films on color in art and color in the daily environment, and by exposing the children to fine reproductions (originals, if possible) of paintings by Henri Matisse, Hans Hoffman, Odilon Redon, Pierre Bonnard, Paul Gauguin, William Turner including also the contemporary styles of R. B. Kitaj, Sam Francis, Mark Rothko, Clifford Still, Paul Jenkins, Morris Louis, Lamar Dodd, and Kenneth Noland.

Build the youngsters' color confidence through assigned projects that involve multicolor choices, for example, the making of 35-mm slide transparencies utilizing discarded color slides, pieces of colored cellophane, colored silk threads, and colored inks; the creation of a color modulator or light mobile employing discarded wire coat hangers, colored pieces of plastic or glass, glass beads, discarded color games (suspend or display against a light source); the construction of a miniature stained glass window utilizing discarded colored or stained glass pieces; the making of a mosaic mural in colored ceramic tile or glass.

We live in a space age. In 1969 American ingenuity, daring, and creativeness put a man on the moon. In 1963 the National Aeronautical and Space Administration commissioned the artist Lamar Dodd to record for posterity the Mercury Astronaut Project space shot at Cape Kennedy, then Cape Canaveral, in Florida. The oil painting on opposite page of a rocket in a gantry is a testimony to the artist's vision, skill, and imagination. The colors sing! It is entitled, "Before Blast Off 130 D." Collection NASA, Washington, D. C.

GRADES ONE AND TWO

The majority of young children enjoy cutting and pasting, so collage projects are especially recommended at this stage. Encourage the youngsters in scissor-cutting skills to create simple shapes out of paper. Afford them opportunities that involve pasting small shapes on large shapes. Talk about creating pattern and contrast by pasting one color over another, one shape over another. Provide hints on using and applying paste economically and effectively. Introduce folded and cut paper design projects. Utilize different colored construction and poster paper backgrounds.

Encourage imaginative themes for individual collage projects, for example: *A Make-Believe Jungle, A Fantastic Garden, A Magic Forest, Fifty-Fathoms Deep, Over the Rainbow, Birds in a Tree.*

Group project murals in the cut-and-paste technique, where each child contributes one or more parts to the whole, are remarkably successful at this grade level. Recommended themes: *The Zoo, The Circus, Tropical Birds, Animals in the Jungle, Butterflies in the Garden, The Pet Show, Disneyland, The Toy Shop, Fish in the Sea, Flu Bugs.* For a detailed description of the group cut-and-paste mural see the section entitled "Making a Mural."

The very young child can manage cutting simple geometric shapes. He must be guided to apply paste economically. Provide a means for storing unfinished collages so children do not have to rush to finish them in one period.

In some instances the felt board can be employed to introduce very young children to the possibilities of cut-out shapes of all sizes and colors, including the many ways they can be juxtaposed and overlapped in a changing composition.

Other suggested themes for individual collage projects: *Land of Make-Believe (Leprechauns, Elves), Creatures from Another World, Birds in a Cage, Autumn Trees, Masks, Imaginative Flags, Children of Other Lands, Kite Designs.*

GRADES THREE AND FOUR

Build on knowledge gained in first and second grade cut-and-paste experiences. Review procedures for cutting, tearing, pasting, and creating pattern or raised surfaces through folding, fringing, pleating, weaving, and curling the paper.

Direct attention now to positive and negative shapes achieved through cutting the paper. Suggest how the negative shape (which is what remains after cutting a positive shape out of a piece of paper) can be utilized in a design as well.

Introduce colored tissue paper, either torn or cut, as a collage element. Most youngsters will now be able to handle the tissue medium quite successfully. Encourage color discoveries by having the children build tissue paper layers, beginning with the lightest colors first. Use white construction paper as background. See section entitled "Tissue Paper Collage."

Group project cut-out and pin-up murals are recommended for these grade levels as well. Subject matter might include: *Cities in Space, Cities at the Bottom of the Sea, The Forest and Its Denizens, The Flower Market, A Kite Festival, Winter Carnival, My Town, Fun in the Snow.*

Suggest cut colored construction or tissue paper designs for notebook covers, canister covers, or placemats. If desired, apply a coat of clear plastic or lacquer to protect the surfaces.

Other suggested themes or ideas for collage include: *Allover Patterns, The Insect World, A Still-Life Arrangement (musical instruments or sports equipment), Posters, Shopping Bags, Umbrellas in the Rain, Number or Letter Designs and Abstract or Nonobjective Designs inspired by sounds: a whisper, a shout, a click, a swish, a hum, a rattle, a squeak, a roar, or a thunder clap.*

GRADES FIVE AND SIX

Recapitulate previous learnings and discoveries, including positive and negative shapes, creating patterns through overlapping or pasting small shapes on large shapes, and suggesting partially three-dimensional effects through folding, fringing, or curling the paper. Introduce paper scoring for students who are ready for further challenges. Demonstrate scoring technique. Place paper to be scored on newspaper padding. Use blunt point of scissors or similar tool and indent curved line desired into paper, then carefully fold along indented line. Be careful not to cut paper when indenting.

Youngsters at this level can master more intricate detail in cutting, but they must be encouraged to complete their big, basic shapes first.

Challenge the students to scout for unusual *found materials* to use in their collages, such as wallpaper and rug samples, fabric remnants, building materials, fur, tarpaper, sandpaper, corrugated paper, old shingles (see Appendix E).

Subject-matter themes for collage projects now can be more complex, more sophisticated. Suggest cityscapes, harbors, still-life arrangements, group-figure studies, and compositions based on abstract motifs or moods, such as *Spring Fever, Traffic Jam, The Blues, Metamorphosis, Roller Derby, Drag Race, Indian Summer, Snowbound, Rock and Roll, Explosion, Lullaby.*

GRADES ONE AND TWO

Young children can be introduced to basic print-making processes from the first grade on. Simple repeat prints resulting in effective allover patterns can be made utilizing vegetables, *found objects,* clay or rubber stamps, cellulose scraps, and, of course, hands and fingers as the imprinting pieces. In most instances colored construction paper is recommended for the background surface. Tempera paint, water-color, or water-base printing ink is suggested for the color-printing medium (see section entitled "Vege-table Prints."

A print may also be taken of a fingerpainting by placing a sheet of newsprint, colored tissue, or col-ored construction paper over the fingerpainting and applying pressure with the palm of the hand or a roller. If the fingerpainting is done on a white for-mica, oilcloth, or glass surface, the monoprint process is an effective way to preserve the painting. The pres-sure of taking the print will alter the painting some-what, often with surprisingly happy results. Do not wait too long to take the print after fingerpainting because the water-base paint dries very quickly. For upper-grade monoprints, oil-base ink, which remains moist longer, is recommended.

Another relatively simple printing technique which can be used to introduce the children to varied linear possibilities is the glue line print (see section entitled "Glue Line Prints").

Vegetable prints appeal to the young child but caution must be exercised in cutting the designs. Use a plastic knife, nails, or melon scoop. Do not insist on the measured design. Grade 2. Iowa City, Iowa.

The printmaking program in the primary grades is limited somewhat because the majority of the young-sters do not possess the needed skills for the com-plicated techniques so often required in producing a print.

Suggested themes for primary-level printmaking: *Free Designs, Self-Portraits, The Animal Kingdom, Birds, Flowers, Fish, Insects, Allover Patterns.*

OPPOSITE PAGE—"Found materials" such as magazine ads can enrich the school's art resources. Here upper-grade youngsters utilized the patterns and colors of magazine pages to create exciting collages. LEFT—Grade 6, Athens, Georgia. RIGHT—Grade 5, Oshkosh, Wisconsin.

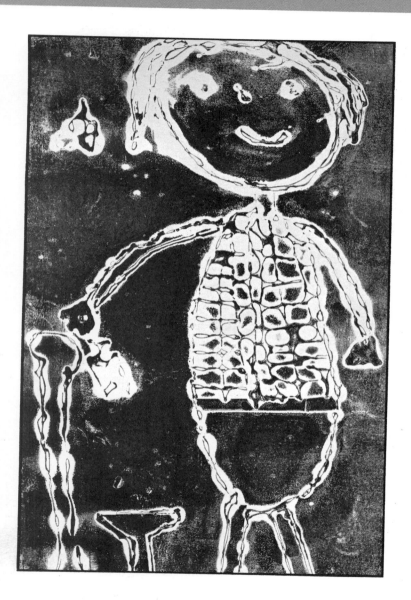

GRADES THREE AND FOUR

The vegetable, clay stamp, and *found object* prints can now be augmented with oil pastel colors as a final embellishment (see section entitled "Vegetable Prints"). If tempera paint has been employed to make the vegetable or *found object* prints, they can be enriched even further. Apply a coat of India ink to the dried print. Allow a few hours for the ink to dry and then wash or rinse off at sink (see section entitled "Tempera Batik").

At this grade level the youngsters can successfully tackle the collograph or cardboard relief print. This is a more challenging and complex print process (see section entitled "Collographs").

Prints involving a linear interpretation are very successful at this level. Recommended techniques include: the glue print; the string print; the soft-plastic-sheet print (indented lines are scored on the commercially available plastic sheet with a blunt-point tool; the sheet is inked with a roller and printed; the indented lines will appear white on black in the final print); the plaster-sheet print (similar in technique to the plastic-sheet print); and the monoprint. It is recommended that only one or two students at a time work on monoprints. A sheet of glass, its edges taped, or a rectangle or square of white formica is inked with a roller. Oil-base ink is recommended. A

LEFT—Glue prints offer the growing child and his classroom teacher a real challenge and extend the printmaking possibilities into exciting, expressive realms. Self portrait. Grade 2, Oshkosh, Wisconsin.

linear composition is made by scratching through the ink surface with a stick, Q-tip, finger, or other tool. A sheet of newsprint or tissue paper is placed over the inked surface and the print is pulled.

Suggested themes for printmaking: *Animals in Their Habitats, Birds in Foliage, Fish in the Sea, A Racing Car, A Clown, Insects and Leaves, Butterflies, Space Ship, The School Bus.*

GRADES FIVE AND SIX

Although the various printmaking techniques of the vegetable print, collograph, and monoprint already introduced in the earlier grades can be repeated at this grade level, augmented now perhaps by more complex compositional motifs, the youngsters of this age will respond to more complicated, more challenging print processes.

Linoleum printing is a favorite with many, especially the boys, because of the opportunity to use hand tools for cutting. Wood-block prints are also popular for similar reasons. Naturally, more materials, more equipment, and more time are required for advanced printmaking. Organization of inking, printing, and clean-up areas is very important (see section entitled "Linoleum Prints").

Other more sophisticated printmaking techniques are possible where special presses are available. These include a lithographic process commercially known as Lithosketch; engravings utilizing acetate or discarded X-ray plates; engravings employing a glossy hard-surfaced cardboard as the plate; and engravings utilizing a polymer-coated cardboard as the plate.

Suggested subjects or themes for printmaking at this level include: *A Still-Life Arrangement of Baseball or Football Gear, Self-Portraits, Portrait of a Classmate, Cityscape, Figure Study from a Model, Animals in Their Habitat, Vintage Automobile, Nature Study of Flowers or Weeds, The Insect World, A Farm Machine, An Open Garage, A Corner of a Workshop.*

RIGHT ABOVE—Monoprint. *Apply fingerpaint or water-base printing ink to sheet of glass (tape edges) or glossy surface cardboard. Make design with fingers or Q-tips into paint. Take print using sheet of newsprint, manila, or construction paper. Combine powder paint and liquid soap to make fingerpaint.*

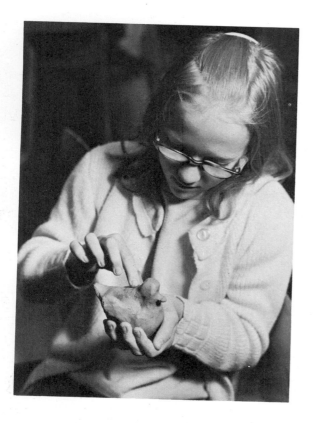

GRADES ONE AND TWO

Provide for one or two exploratory experiences in clay. It is important that sufficient clay be available (a ball of clay approximately the size of a grapefruit for each child is recommended) and that it be of the proper consistency, malleable, clean, not too wet, not to dry. Check the condition of the clay a day or two before the clay project begins, unless, of course, commercially prepared moist clay is used.

Allow the youngsters to discover the potential of the clay during the initial exploratory sessions. Encourage squeezing, pinching, poking, coil-making, and forming clay into balls. Guide the children in creating familiar forms or objects in clay.

Suggest to the youngsters that they hold the ball or lump of clay in their cupped hands while they manipulate it into the desired form. This technique discourages the tendency of many children to pound the clay on their desk into a flat, two-dimensional slab.

Most children enjoy creating animals and birds in clay. They discover that they can control the relatively simple sculptural demands of a rabbit, elephant, turtle, cow, bear, pig, hippo, bird nesting, horse, or dinosaur.

TOP—Encourage youngsters to hold the clay in their hands when making three-dimensional ceramic forms. BOTTOM—Children can manage fairly successful pinch pots but the technique must be discussed with them.

54

The teacher may schedule a field trip to a farm, zoo, animal shelter, or natural museum where the children can find inspiration for their clay expression. The clay modeling itself should be preceded by a discussion centering around the characteristic aspects of the animals or birds the children have selected to depict. Clay lends itself well to group projects where each child contributes one animal or figure. Themes such as *The Farm, The Zoo, Noah's Ark, The Circus* are very popular with the youngsters.

Children at this stage can also construct simple pinch pots. With a lump of clay the size of an orange, plus the following instructions, the children can manage a fairly successful pot which may be bisque fired, if desired. Insert thumb into the middle of the clay ball. Rotate the clay ball in the palm of one hand, as you push and pinch thumb and fingers of the other hand along the ball in overlapping pinches. Do not make wall of the pot too thin. Allow the marks of the thumb and fingers to remain. Fire if kiln facilities are available. Simple, subtle glazes are recommended if available.

For many schools the firing and glazing of children's clay creations is not practical because of limited facilities. These beautiful glazed ceramic animals are by a gifted youngster from Burns Park School. Grade 1, Ann Arbor, Michigan.

55

GRADES THREE AND FOUR

Review with the children what they have learned about clay—its plasticity, its possibilities, its limitations. An introductory, exploratory session in clay manipulation is again recommended. Previous knowledge about clay should be recapitulated as children work. As they share ideas, the teacher might make a chalkboard record of their discoveries. They will probably recall that hard clay is difficult to model; that soft clay sags if the supports are not strong enough; that appendages break off when clay dries unless they are securely fastened to the main structure; that textures and patterns can be made in clay with fingers, pencils, and assorted *found objects*.

In making clay animals the post and lintel technique is usually recommended (see section entitled "Clay" for a detailed description of this process). This basic structure can then be manipulated, turned, modeled, added to, condensed, or stretched until the youngster achieves the characteristic body form he desires.

Youngsters at this stage can explore more complex techniques in pottery making. The simple pinch pot may now be augmented by directions for making the double pinch pot container. Remind the youngsters, too, about scoring and slip-cementing procedures.

TOP—Youngster using the post and lintel approach in constructing and modeling a dinosaur. BOTTOM—Clay prehistorical animal. The post and lintel building approach was used. Adaptations were made as the work progressed.

56

GRADES FIVE AND SIX

Review facts about clay and clay manipulation. Provide for a period of clay exploration and let children share discoveries made concerning clay in previous grades, its possibilities and its limitations.

More complex ceramic modeling may now be attempted. Popular subject matter themes include legendary figures, Biblical heroes, horse and rider, animals and their young, portraits, animals in combat, family pets, and mother with child interpretations. Youngsters will now place a strong emphasis on achieving correct proportions, action, and detail. The teacher must be prepared to offer guidance when necessary. In most situations refer the student to the inspirational source of the subject matter—the figure or animal itself, to a film, or to an excellent photograph or color slide. Neither praise the purely naturalistic approach so often admired by the growing youngster nor criticize it; instead, introduce the student to those approaches, techniques, and interpretations that are aesthetically more expressive, more restrained, and more universal. Obtain and exhibit reproductions, either in color or black and white, of ceramic sculpture from ancient cultures—Chinese Tang figurines, Japanese Jomon and Haniwa figures, pots in the form of human figures from Mexico and Peru, especially the expressive creations of the Tarascans.

In the area of pottery-making the children can progress from the simple pinch pots of the early grades, to the more complicated combined pinch or coil containers of the intermediate grades, and then to more complex and challenging slab-and-patch techniques. Actually, all approaches in pot-making can be combined to produce expressive, functional pottery (see section entitled "Clay").

Ancient ceramic Haniwa horse from Japan. "Haniwa" describes the hollow clay cylinders that were used in the basic construction. Note the simplicity and directness of execution. Notice, too, how clay coils have been flattened and used to add functional and decorative embellishments.

GRADES ONE AND TWO

Youngsters who are growing in the vocabulary and language of art usually are more successful in their art endeavors. The teacher should utilize the chalkboard to call their attention to project-related art words such as art, balance, black, blue, brown, brush, cardboard, chalk, circle, clay, coil, color, composition, construction paper, crayon, dark, design, dot, drawing, easel, engraving, fingerpaint, glue, green, gray, hammer, kiln, light, line, manila paper, mobile, modeling, mural, nail, newsprint, orange, oval, overlapping, paste, pastel, pattern, pen, pencil, pin, pinch pot, plaid, prism, purple, rectangle, red, repetition, ruler, scribble, sculpture, shape, square, stripe, tagboard, tempera paint, texture, tissue paper, triangle, variety, watercolor, weaving, white, yellow.

GRADES THREE AND FOUR

The following words should become part of the youngster's growing art vocabulary in addition to those recommended for grades 1 and 2: background, balsa wood, bas relief, batik, brayer, carbon paper, ceramics, chipboard, collage, collograph, complementary colors, cone, contrast, contour line, corrugated paper, cube, cylinder, detail, enamel, foreground, form, *found materials,* gouge, gum eraser, hue, incised relief, India ink, inking slab, intensity, landscape, linoleum, linoprint, masking tape, masonite, monoprint, mosaic, negative shape, opaque, papier-mâché, plaster, plywood, positive shape, poster, poster board, pyramid, radiation, railroad board, rasp, relief, rubber cement, scoring, shade, shellac, sketch, slab (clay), slip (clay), spectrum, stabile, staple, still life, stitchery, tie and dye, tint, translucent, transparent, turpentine, unity, value, wash drawing, wedging (clay).

GRADES FIVE AND SIX

Build on the art vocabulary developed in previous grades. Augment with the following new words: abstract art, acetate, acrylics, aesthetic, analogous, armature, arrangement, *assemblage,* asymmetry, baren, black light, branch pot, burnish, cartoon, charcoal, chroma, conte crayon, converging lines, crosshatch, distortion, dowel, encaustic, engobe, etching, Expressionism, firebrick, fixative, foamglass, foreshortening, frottage, gesture drawing, glaze, greenware, grog, grout, *happening,* horizon line, Impressionism, indigo, kneaded eraser, lacquer, leather-hard clay, linear, mass, medium, mixed media, mold, monochromatic, montage, motif, neutralization, Nonobjective Art, ochre, Op Art, palette, paraffin, patina, perspective, plaster bat, polymer medium, Pop Art, press, proportion, Q-tip, raffia, reed, repoussé, scratch pen, Sculpmetal, sepia, shading, sienna, sloyd knife, solder, Surrealism, symbol, symmetry, tension, terra cotta clay, tessera, tracing paper, umber, vanishing point, vermiculite, wood block, X-acto knife.

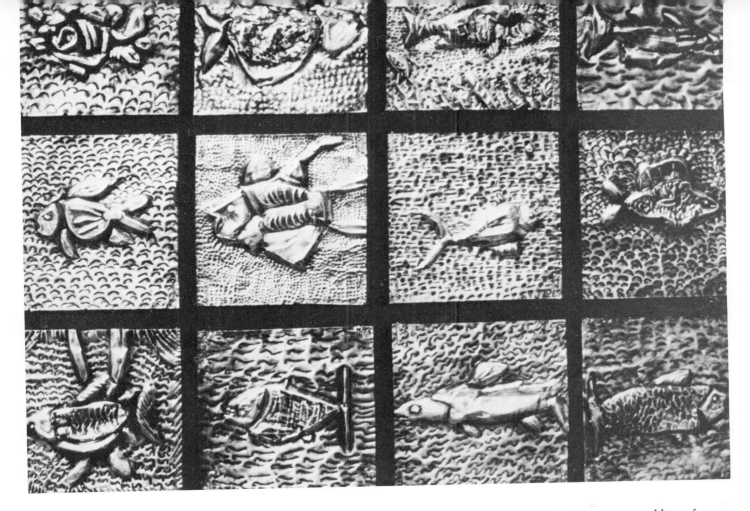

Metal embossing or tooling is an art project upper-grade youngsters really enjoy. See examples on this page by Milwaukee elementary school children. The teacher should provide exciting visual motivation and resources so youngsters can make their own creative designs. Discourage use of molds or stereotype patterns. Suggest they make preliminary drawing in pencil on notebooks, newsprint, or manila paper in the same size as the metal sheet they have chosen to emboss. Fish, insects, birds, reptiles, jungle animals, and their own pets are popular as subject matter themes. Heavy weight aluminum foil wrap or commercially available aluminum sheeting (36 or 40 gauge) is recommended. Tape preliminary drawing to metal sheet or let children use it as a guide for direct embossing. Use a generous padding of newspaper under the metal sheet during the actual tooling or embossing. For making the relief indentations use a blunt pencil, a ball point pen, the end of a watercolor brush, or commercially available wooden modeling tools. Be careful not to employ a tool sharp enough to cut through the thin metal sheet. When the metal design is embossed, you may embellish it further by giving it a coat of India ink, allowing it to dry, then burnishing it with fine-grain steel wool to bring out the highlights. If the budget allows, you can order thin copper sheeting, emboss it, and give it a special subtle patina with liver of sulphur. Embossed projects can be attractively mounted on wood panels.

59

6

A PROGRAM IN ACTION

A number of projects and techniques in two and three dimensions recommended for a qualitative elementary school art program are described in detail on the following pages. The presentations should prove most helpful to classroom teachers who are very often unskilled in the basic art processes of painting, print-making, collage, sculpture, and crafts. Elementary school teachers generally know a great deal about the children in their classes, their characteristics, and their behavior but too often their knowledge of the motivational strategies and the evaluative procedures they must employ to help the child in art is not their strongest area of competence.

The following descriptions of art projects in action encompass both the practical and theoretical aspects of the unit or lesson. They state motivational possibilities, they clarify complex techniques, they offer solutions for organizational and supply problems, and they suggest applications of reasonable, attainable art criteria.

In no instance is the implication intended, nor is the reader to assume, that these approaches or guidelines are the only ones possible, but for the record, they have been tried and found highly successful in situation after situation in today's typically crowded elementary schools, in classrooms filled with eager, bright, dreamy, fidgety, sleepy, tired, energetic, noisy, apathetic, boisterous, talkative, individual, and wonderful children. The illustrations of the projects speak for themselves.

A dynamic, developmental art program in the elementary school should provide a variety of in-depth art experiences. Youngsters who sometimes have difficulty in one technique may blossom in another. The illustrations on opposite page include only a fraction of the colorful projects and related activities that a qualitative curriculum in art should include.

in two 50-minute art periods. Grade 1, Athens, Georgia.

As the children draw, guide them to look at the figure carefully, to get their eyes full. Caution them against rushing, scribbling, or making hasty, lazy lines. Tell them to look first, then draw. Remind them to make the figure large, to fill the page with it so that their classmates can see it from across the room. Sometimes it is helpful if they begin their drawing of a figure starting with the head at the top of the page.

Figure drawing, as all drawing from life, teaches the child to be observant in many ways. It is amazing how quickly the growing, discerning child notices embellishing details such as belts, ribbons, shoelaces, buttons, necklaces, bracelets, pockets, insignia, ruffles, pleats, glasses, belts, or the pattern of clothes, such as stripes, dots, diamonds, and plaids, using them to enrich his interpretation.

Figure drawing from the model, especially in the upper grades, can often lead to utilization of the figure or group of figures in a painting, collage, print, or group mural.

However, the preliminary sketches themselves, either in pencil, pen, or crayon, have a validity and integrity of their own. Subject matter themes such as *I am playing ball, I am riding a bike, I am skipping rope, I am playing a guitar* lend themselves effectively to space-filling compositions.

64

Motivation for drawing and painting is more meaningful when students identify with the subject drawn. Here young-sters used mixed media of crayon, watercolor, and pastel to create these figure compositions. Grade 6, Athens, Georgia.

6

A PROGRAM IN ACTION

A number of projects and techniques in two and three dimensions recommended for a qualitative elementary school art program are described in detail on the following pages. The presentations should prove most helpful to classroom teachers who are very often unskilled in the basic art processes of painting, print-making, collage, sculpture, and crafts. Elementary school teachers generally know a great deal about the children in their classes, their characteristics, and their behavior but too often their knowledge of the motivational strategies and the evaluative procedures they must employ to help the child in art is not their strongest area of competence.

The following descriptions of art projects in action encompass both the practical and theoretical aspects of the unit or lesson. They state motivational possibilities, they clarify complex techniques, they offer solutions for organizational and supply problems, and they suggest applications of reasonable, attainable art criteria.

In no instance is the implication intended, nor is the reader to assume, that these approaches or guidelines are the only ones possible, but for the record, they have been tried and found highly successful in situation after situation in today's typically crowded elementary schools, in classrooms filled with eager, bright, dreamy, fidgety, sleepy, tired, energetic, noisy, apathetic, boisterous, talkative, individual, and wonderful children. The illustrations of the projects speak for themselves.

A dynamic, developmental art program in the elementary school should provide a variety of in-depth art experiences. Youngsters who sometimes have difficulty in one technique may blossom in another. The illustrations on opposite page include only a fraction of the colorful projects and related activities that a qualitative curriculum in art should include.

DRAWING THE FIGURE

What skills, what techniques in figure drawing should be introduced and developed in the elementary school art program? What can teachers actually say to the child about the delineation of the figure? When, if ever, should relative proportions of the human figure be emphasized? These are a few of the critical questions involving figure drawing that confront the elementary teacher. Unfortunately, the strategy most often proposed is "Let the child alone. He will find his own way," which usually provides the classroom teacher with a face-saving excuse if the results are less than satisfactory. However, this is hardly the advice given to teachers regarding other subject areas.

LEFT—Figure drawing from the posed model in class. Felt tip pen or marker. Grade 3. TOP—Black crayon drawing. Grade 2.

If teachers want the child to grow in expressing himself through his representation of the figure, then they must provide learning experiences and practice sessions for such growth. Fortunately, there are some avenues a teacher can pursue to help children develop confidence in figure drawing. Youngsters can become more aware of the human figure and its characteristics by observing the posed model in class at every grade level. If children in the primary school draw the figure in their pictures, they have no doubt observed it on various occasions to enable them to put down their impressions of it. The delineation of the figure in even the youngest child's drawings does not emerge out of a vacuum. What is wrong then with the close attention, the immediate perception and identification with the figure that the posed model offers?

Before the students actually begin drawing, a warm-up session is recommended. Motivating or leading questions should be asked. What is the posed figure doing? What part of the figure do you see from where you are? What is the figure wearing? How big is the figure's head in comparison to the body? How big are the hands? Put your hand over your face. Did you realize your hands were so big? How big are the feet? They must be large enough to keep us steady as we walk. Where is the arm the largest? At the shoulder or at the wrist? Where is the leg the largest? At the ankle or near the hips? Where does the body, the leg, or the arm bend? How wide can the feet stretch apart? How high can the arm reach above the head? How far can the body swing around?

"Fun on the Playground." The children took turns modeling for their classmates. The drawings in white chalk on colored construction paper grew figure by figure, pose by pose in one class session. The coloring in oil pastel was completed in two 50-minute art periods. Grade 1, Athens, Georgia.

63

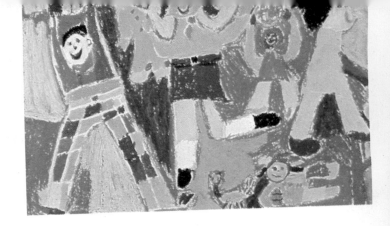

As the children draw, guide them to look at the figure carefully, to get their eyes full. Caution them against rushing, scribbling, or making hasty, lazy lines. Tell them to look first, then draw. Remind them to make the figure large, to fill the page with it so that their classmates can see it from across the room. Sometimes it is helpful if they begin their drawing of a figure starting with the head at the top of the page.

Figure drawing, as all drawing from life, teaches the child to be observant in many ways. It is amazing how quickly the growing, discerning child notices embellishing details such as belts, ribbons, shoelaces, buttons, necklaces, bracelets, pockets, insignia, ruffles, pleats, glasses, belts, or the pattern of clothes, such as stripes, dots, diamonds, and plaids, using them to enrich his interpretation.

Figure drawing from the model, especially in the upper grades, can often lead to utilization of the figure or group of figures in a painting, collage, print, or group mural.

However, the preliminary sketches themselves, either in pencil, pen, or crayon, have a validity and integrity of their own. Subject matter themes such as *I am playing ball, I am riding a bike, I am skipping rope, I am playing a guitar* lend themselves effectively to space-filling compositions.

64

Motivation for drawing and painting is more meaningful when students identify with the subject drawn. Here youngsters used mixed media of crayon, watercolor, and pastel to create these figure compositions. Grade 6, Athens, Georgia.

These contour drawings are by Japanese children. Observe the delineation of the wood paneling and the boys' socks and shoes, not to mention the fingernails. Grades 5 and 6.

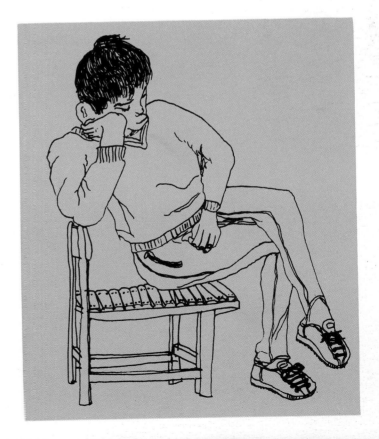

In projects where figure drawing is involved, many classroom teachers feel they lack the necessary expertise to guide the youngsters with confidence. They often settle, therefore, for what the children can accomplish on their own without any guidance whatsoever. But what about the child himself? Shouldn't he receive as much help in this activity as he gets in math or science? The wrong kind of direction, however, is not the answer either. Stereotyped formulas such as stick figures, proportions measured by rule, and other conforming devices should be avoided at all costs.

Basic motivating and teaching strategies for primary school figure drawing have been suggested earlier. Tested and proven approaches in figure delineation to whet the interest of the upper-grade youngster follow:

Utilize a student model in a colorful costume or sports uniform.

Pose the model in the center of a circle of students.

Introduce new drawing and sketching tools such as the free-flowing felt-tipped or nylon-tipped pens and markers, ball-point pens, sticks, and India ink.

Pose the student model against a sheet of cardboard, approximately 4 by 8 feet, in any case slightly larger than the model. This will help the youngsters relate the posed figure to the boundaries of their paper.

Demonstrate new approaches in drawing the figure: contour, gesture, scribble, mass. In contour drawing the student is instructed to look intently at the model as he draws and to refer to his sketch or paper only at critical junctures.

Suggest a pose with more than one student taking part. Pose the model in conjunction with a still-life arrangement.

Challenge the students to use their imaginations in drawing. Let the action or stance of the figure trigger a theme or idea for them.

Have different models take 5-minute turns in posing, playing ball, cheerleading, and dancing, and recommend that students overlap the figures as they draw, using a different colored crayon for each pose.

Vary the size of the paper the children use for sketching. Try some narrow 6″ × 12″ or 12″ × 24″ sheets for standing or reclining poses, some square 12″ × 12″ or 18″ × 18″ paper for crouching or sitting poses.

If you have sufficient space in your classroom, give the youngsters the opportunity to work on large 24″ × 36″ paper with large brushes or large chunk charcoal.

Introduce a variety of papers to draw on: plain newsprint, Manila, white drawing, assorted colored construction, brown wrapping, bogus, or classified ad pages from the daily news.

Let the youngsters try the cut or torn paper technique in their interpretation of the figure. In this method they look at the model and cut or tear directly without any preliminary drawing.

Older children might benefit from the use of resource material, such as a real skeleton, so they could study bone structure and junctures.

Inexpensive, lightweight 18″ × 24″ drawing boards can be constructed of ¼″ or ⅛″ chipboard, cardboard, Upson, or beaverboard. The edges of these boards can be protected with overlapping ½″ masking tape. During the drawing session, these boards can be tilted against table or desk giving the child a better working position from which to observe the model.

Youngsters enjoy modeling for their classmates. Respect the wishes, however, of those who object to doing it. Art class in action at University School, Oshkosh, Wisconsin, and Briarcliff Elementary School, Atlanta, Georgia. Grade 5.

67

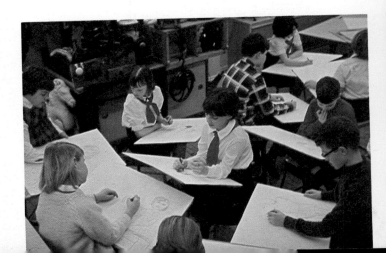

For action or gesture drawing which requires a free approach, the children should be encouraged to hold the crayon, pencil, or chalk horizontally as they sketch rather than upright as in writing.

Promote self-identification through figure drawing experiences that have meaning for the youngsters: playing a musical instrument, riding a bike or motorcycle, performing a dance, cheerleading, playing football, basketball, baseball, tennis, standing under an umbrella in the rain, balancing on a fence or rail, skipping rope, twirling a baton, diving into a pool, jumping on a trampoline, casting for a fish, romping with a dog.

LEFT—Rich experience, sensitive perception, and keen observation helped this gifted youngster describe a visit to the beauty shop. Note the tears. Grade 4, Winona, Minnesota.

TOP—"Brushing my teeth and combing my hair." Grade 1. Note the four eyeballs—two for watching the toothbrush and two for watching the hairbrush!

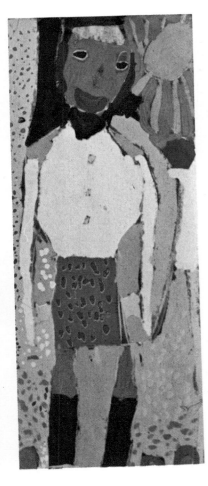  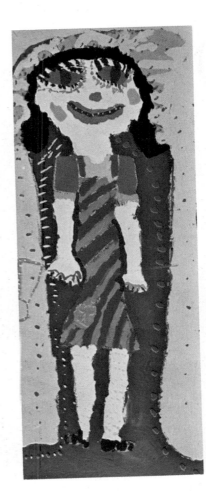 

These colorful tempera figure paintings prove again how truly individual youngsters can be in their art expression even though the materials are the same, and the assigned theme similar—in this case, "A Portrait of My Classmate." Here again the qualitative, in-depth strategies are revealed, the preparation and patience necessary to mix a varied range of hues, the time taken to make a preliminary sketch and to make deliberate, sensitive choices in applying colors—all are evident in the final results. Grade 3, Oshkosh, Wisconsin.

Illustrations on following two pages are progress drawings in black crayon on manila paper. Subject: "Brushing my teeth or combing my hair." Note how early base line disappears—how floor moves up to meet baseboard. Notice how the face in the mirror appears at Grade 5, and the concern with details. Approximate time: 50 minutes.

James, age six.

Jimmy, age seven.

Jeff, age nine.

Linda Kay, age six.

Janice, age eight.

Jane, age eight.

Loren, age ten.

John, age ten.

Halli, age nine.

Kathy, age ten.

Kathy, age eleven.

DRAWING THE LANDSCAPE

While very young children in the primary grades enjoy drawing simple themes and single objects such as a house, butterfly, car, tree, or animal, growing youngsters respond to the challenge of the complex landscape or cityscape, to the visual interrelationships in their environment. They are now more interested in outdoor sketching and the excitement of field trips. The busy and infinitely varied world beckons and un-folds at their very doorsteps:

    The building construction down the street
    The perspective down an alley
    The colorful shopping center
    The big city skyscrapers
    The county fairgrounds
    The cluster of farm houses on a country plain
    The city park and bandstand
    The courthouse square
    The service station
    The bus, train, and airport terminals
    The boat marina
    The school building and yard
    The harbor with its ships
    The factories and foundries
    The view from a classroom or bedroom window

The most ordinary scene can become the inspiration for an expressive drawing.

These and countless other sights can become the inspiration for their sketches, their compositions, their paintings. A variety of media can be used for outdoor sketching: pencil, charcoal, ball point pen, felt-nib marker, stick and ink, chalk, or crayon.

Many youngsters on sketching field trips draw with confidence, but some besiege the teacher with such perplexing questions as: "What should I draw first?" "Should I start at the top of the page?" "Should I put everything in?"

Sometimes the complex view overwhelms them. Sometimes the spatial and perspective problems confuse them. Fortunately there are proven approaches to landscape and cityscape drawing that teachers have found worthwhile in guiding children. In one strategy, the teacher recommends that the child begin with a light pencil or chalk sketch to establish the basic shapes. Once the youngster has established his outline, he can develop details and value.

Another technique that is quite successful, especially when the view is complex, is to suggest that the child begin with some shape in the center of the site—a doorway, perhaps, a telephone pole, a window, a tree, a silo, a small section of a building—draw it as completely as he can, then proceed to draw the shape above it and below it, to the right and left of it, and so on until he fills the page and touches the borders of his paper. He will find that incomplete shapes will form avenues into his composition. Then guide him to continue his drawing, adding detail, pattern, textures, and shadow as he desires.

TOP—Landscape composition by young girl sketching at site (see opposite page). Black crayon and white chalk on gray manila paper made possible a wide range of monochromatic values. Learning to look intently is important in drawing. BOTTOM—Felt marker drawing made at site. Grade 4. See next page.

73

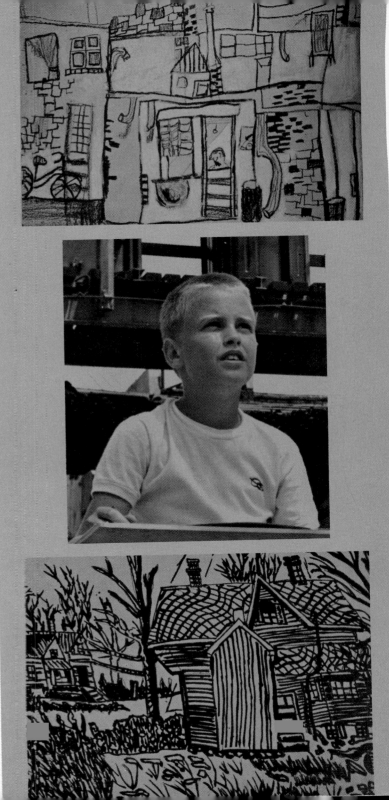

Problems youngsters have with defining distance often can be clarified by an understanding of the following guidelines:

Objects or shapes in foreground, or closer to the observer, are usually drawn larger and lower on the page.

Objects farther away from observer, or in the background, are usually drawn smaller and higher on the page.

An effective space is created by overlapping shapes, such as a fence or tree against a building.

Simple perspective principles, based on the use of the horizon line, vanishing points, and converging lines, should be introduced only when the youngster indicates a need for them.

Sketching field trips should be undertaken only with adequate planning and preparation on the part of teacher and students. If possible, exciting subject matter should be scouted by the teacher beforehand. Avoid barren views or monotonous vistas that provide little opportunity for contrasting and varied space break-up.

A class discussion prior to the field trip or sketching excursion is a means of emphasizing specific challenges in advance. Things to look for might include:

Take time to scout for varied, interesting sites in the school vicinity where older students could find stimulating material to draw on sketching excursions. BOTTOM—Youngster makes drawing of her house from memory after a recall session.

the mood or atmosphere of the site, the unique or significant characteristics of the buildings, the problems to be solved in drawing perspective views, the effect of darker window panes in daylight, the foreground space allowed for steps and porches, suggestions for making receding fences or walls stand straight and sidewalks lie flat, and varied means for effective break-up of foreground and background.

The teacher may remind the students that in drawing the landscape or cityscape they may use the artist's creative prerogatives of changing, adding, deleting, or simplifying what they see at the site. The criterion is not photographic reality nor measured perspective. If the student wishes, he may add more trees, telephone poles, air vents or windows; he may change a roof line or the cast of a shadow; he may ignore and delete a parked car or a poster on a wall. Each decision he makes, however, should be colored by design considerations so that the final composition embodies unity through effective juxtaposition of elements, repetition of shapes, sensitively observed details, directional lines, overlapping of forms, textural interests, a variety of positive and negative areas and spaces, and an exciting balance of darks and light values.

Japanese elementary school children are fortunate. Art is scheduled 2 hours each week. They learn to mix paints on a palette from the first grade on. These sensitive paintings by sixth-grade youngsters from Japan are the result of in-depth experiences in art.

75

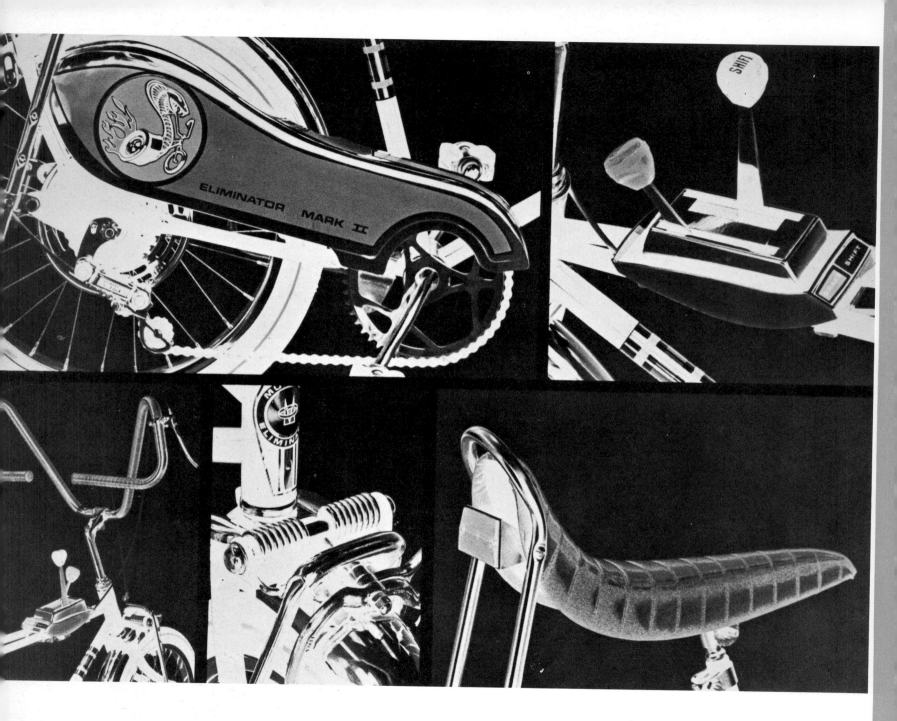

DRAWING THE STILL LIFE

The still-life arrangement, whether as inspiration for drawing, painting, print, or collage, is an especially effective means of encouraging keen observation and awareness, developing sensitive perception, emphasizing varietal delineation of shapes, achieving space through overlapping of objects, and providing the added bonus of initiating an *uncommon* interest in *common*, everyday implements. Children from the first grade on can be encouraged to discover beauty of design and form in the ordinary bottles, teapots, lanterns, clocks, musical instruments, kitchen utensils, and machines that compose the typical still-life.

From the third or fourth grade on, children can be guided to see the varied design possibilities in their still-life compositions. The best still-life arrangements are similar in many respects to complex cityscapes—a grouping of buildings echoing a cluster of bottles, etc.—and they offer related compositional challenges.

The "still life" is all around us. It is not invented or artificial. We live in a world of "still life" arrangements—the classroom itself, the piled-up desk top, the open garage or closet, the box of playground equipment in the principal's office—all are natural everyday "still lifes." *Mixed media collage. Grade 6.*

78

In selecting objects for a still-life arrangement, teachers should choose a variety of *found items*: small, short, tall, simple, complex, organic, textured, and plain. Antique shops, secondhand stores, basements, army surplus warehouses, rummage sales, flea markets, and attics can provide rich sources for unusual and visually stimulating objects that can contribute to exciting still-life groupings. Avoid the trite, miniature figurine or vase as elements in the still-life.

The placement of the various objects is very critical to the ultimate success of the composition or design. Arrange them, for example, on an antique table, old sewing machine, rocker, or chair; on a step ladder; a window ledge; a desk top; or on the floor in the middle of the classroom where the children can be seated in a circle as they draw. Utilize a variety of heights or levels (use cardboard cartons as supports); plan overlapping items and an informal or off-sided balance. Use assorted fabrics, colorful beach towels, fish nets, bedspreads, or tablecloths as drapery to unify the separate elements or to suggest movement from one object to another. For qualitative results, it is recommended that all students be afforded a clear and fairly close view of the still-life arrangement.

OPPOSITE PAGE. LEFT—*Crayon on construction paper. Grade 1.* CENTER—*Tissue collage on white paper over permanent ink drawing. Grade 3.* RIGHT—*Watercolor. Grade 4. This page. Found materials collage. Grade 4.*

In most instances, the more objects that are used in a still-life grouping, provided, of course, that they are arranged at different levels and with varied negative and positive shape exploitation, the more opportunities the youngsters have for selection and rejection. In the same vein, the more objects the children utilize in their compositions, the more effective and richly they fill the pictorial space and build their designs.

There is no one way for youngsters to begin drawing the still-life, as veteran teachers have discovered. One strategy, however, that children respond to, and have success with, follows: They begin carefully by drawing first the central object of the still-life from their point of view in the middle of their paper. They then continue drawing the next object to it, above it, below it, left and right of it, and so on, until they have filled the page. This means, of course, that the more varied and complex the still-life itself, the more space-filling the drawing will be.

Another tactic is to have the students select items from a general store of still-life material, choosing one object at a time to sketch, building their compositions gradually, employing the principles of variety, overlapping, repetition, and informal balance.

Some teachers recommend to their students that they make a light, tentative sketch in pencil, charcoal, or brush and ink to obtain a general, allover composition. This preliminary drawing is then developed, stage by stage, utilizing value (light and dark) effects, pattern, texture, shading, and linear emphasis.

TOP—Collage employing pages from discarded wallpaper sample books. Grade 6. CENTER—Crayon engraving. Crayon applied richly in related warm colors. Black tempera coating. Grade 5. BOTTOM—Mixed media collage. Grade 6, Athens, Georgia.

Uppergrade youngsters look at everyday objects with new understanding when they draw them seriously and perceptively. Widen their horizons by introducing them to exciting artifacts and antiques as subject matter for art expression. A coffee grinder, a railroad lantern, an old mantle clock, a steam iron, or an ancient sewing machine takes on new dimensions through drawing. Discover your own Americana items, then share them with your students through art!

DRAWING ANIMALS

Most children respond quite favorably to drawing experiences where pets and other animals are the subject in question. Girls at the upper elementary school level are especially interested in drawing horses. However, if the drawing of animals is to be a rewarding and valid experience for these youngsters, opportunities for observing a variety of live animals must be provided first.

The teacher can help by arranging field trips to zoos, aquariums, and natural museums. Equally exciting opportunities to observe animals in action or at rest can be found at horse and dog shows, circuses, parades, farms, state or county fairs, animal shelters, or national parks. Pets brought to class provide still another immediate source of drawing inspiration.

Pencil, stick and ink, and nylon-point pens are recommended for small-sized sketches. Charcoal, chalk, crayon, oil pastel, and blunt-nib ink markers can be used effectively on larger compositions. Drawing surfaces suggested include newsprint, cream or gray manila paper, colored construction paper, brown Kraft or butcher paper, and classified sections of newspapers. A simple, effective yet inexpensive drawing board can be constructed out of the side of a large cardboard carton. However, commercially available Upson or beaverboard, 1/4 inch thick, cut into rectangles 18 by 24 inches and edged with masking tape, is especially recommended. These boards could also be used as drawing surfaces on the limited-sized classroom desks.

An animal drawing experience might begin with a field trip to a zoo. Prior to the excursion, the teacher and children could discuss the special characteristics of zoo animals. They might point out the unique features of the various species—their stance, action, disposition, and special physical attributes. Attention might be called, for example, to the textural pattern of the thick-skinned rhino, the wrinkled and leathery face of the orangutan, the repeated yet varied spots of the leopard, the rhythmic rings on the armadillo, the subtle variations of the zebra's stripes, and the gracefully curved horns of the antelope.

When the youngsters begin sketching, they should be encouraged to draw rather generous forms which make the wisest use of the paper's proportions. The larger the drawing, the more opportunities the student has to define and exploit details and textures.

These life drawings might be limited to a delineation of significant details, to an expressive line sketch that might capture the spirit of the animal, rather than to attempt a completed study. Many of the refinements and textural nuances can be added later when the children return to the classroom.

It is recommended that older children on sketching excursions limit their drawing to a single animal, developing the study in-depth. This practice is more beneficial than attempts to draw several different animals in the limited time usually allowed. If scheduling permits, the teacher may plan subsequent visits so that the youngsters will have ample opportunity

84

TOP—Youngsters making sketches of dinosaurs. Note how one child makes a single bold drawing, while his classmate, more prolific, fills his page with several linear interpretations. No two children create or progress in the same manner. BOTTOM—Compare this rhinoceros with Durer's on page 86. Grade 6, Iowa City, Iowa.

1515
RHINOCERVS

*Wood engraving by the German artist Albrecht Dürer,
noted for his animal studies. The youngsters should also be
shown his beautiful drawings of a hare and squirrels.*

to sketch different animals. The student might also attempt separate detailed studies of the animal's eye, ear, tail, hoof, snout, or horns.

The teacher might also suggest that the students draw their animals in some characteristic action such as eating, resting, climbing, bathing, walking, running, or feeding their young. Older children can be challenged to note the individual stance of an animal: the swinging rhythm of a chimpanzee, the arching stretch of a giraffe, the sway of the elephant's trunk, the nervous tension of a horse's legs—all serve as clues to the interpretation of the animal's spirit and disposition.

Careful, deliberate observation and sensitive handling of the drawn line are two fundamental requirements in animal drawings. For inspiration let the youngsters look at these noted animal drawings: Rembrandt's lion and elephant; Delacroix's horses; Durer's squirrel, hare, and rhinoceros; Wyeth's birds; Sosen's monkeys; and Saito's cats.

Drawing or sketching from the animal itself is the primary recommendation. But, when this prospect is out of the question, supplemental motivation, including color slides, films, filmstrips, opaque projections of magazine and book illustrations and photos provided by zoos, educational services, and governmental conservation agencies, will provide vicarious enrichment. In the primary grades, the visual material might be referred to briefly and then the illustrations tacked to the bulletin board for further reference.

TOP—Drawing by Rembrandt van Rijn. CENTER—Youngster concentrates on his drawing. Grade 3, Ann Arbor, Michigan. BOTTOM—Woodblock by Kiyoshi Saito, contemporary Japanese artist. Note how the composition fills the space and how the grain of the woodblock itself has become part of the design.

Mounted photographs fulfill a definite need, but it should be explained to the students that *photos are for inspirational and informational reference only and not for copying or tracing.*

The youngsters need to be reminded, also, to consider the whole composition in their animal drawings. In too many instances, the animal is just drawn in the middle of the paper without any reference to the possibilities of interesting negative space. To help the students in this respect, the teacher might initiate a discussion on the handling of picture space, including the introduction of additional elements to enrich the composition: trees, hills, streams, marshes, cliffs, clouds, other animals in the background or foreground. Environmental supplements such as these can be employed to enhance the main subject and create dynamic positive-negative breakup in the drawing.

Unusual and interesting plants, dried foliage, rocks, or flowers in season can serve as reference material for the animal's habitat. Leaves, plants, and rocks from the immediate school vicinity might be drawn giant-size to become jungle trees and vines with the pattern of the foliage complementing the textures and shapes of the animals themselves.

Both in the classroom and on supervised field trips the child should be provided with many opportunities

to draw directly from nature's sources. Through these perception-building experiences, the youngster learns to sharpen his visual responses and to increase his visual field. As he draws in linear form those images, those phenomena that impress and excite him, he is learning and expressing himself at the same time—a dual achievement.

A mounted owl served as the inspiration for this delightful, sensitive drawing by an upper-grade youngster. Notice the attention given to the fine feather texture. Madison County Schools, Georgia. OPPOSITE PAGE—Children and their pets can often trigger a very personal art expression as these drawings prove. Grade 4, University Elementary School. Oshkosh, Wisconsin.

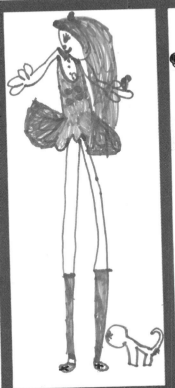

PAINTING WITH TEMPERA

Every child should have the opportunity to express his ideas in paint, whether in tempera, poster colors, or the new polymer mediums. Tempera pigments, if of the best quality, are rich in color, have excellent coverage, and are packaged in functional, nonbreakable containers. Children who paint with tempera can apply color over color freely to achieve special effects or repaint areas they are not satisfied with.

Though classroom teachers are often aware of the many possibilities for art expression that tempera paint provides, they often do not include it in their art program because of the housekeeping chores involved. It is true that tempera projects require more materials preparation, more careful storage, and more expeditious clean-up procedures than watercolor or crayon art; these factors, however, should not prevent teachers from discovering how it can enrich the lives of the children in their classes.

TOP LEFT—*Tempera painting, "Birds in a Tree." Grade 2, Oshkosh, Wisconsin.* TOP RIGHT—*Youngsters learn to share paints available on a paint cart.* BOTTOM—*Tempera. "A Monster." Grade 4, Athens, Georgia.*

In recent years, inventive teachers and art consultants have developed many ways to solve the problems of tempera painting where large classes and limited facilities are involved. Some strategies have proven most effective and time-saving. Discarded baby-food cans and half-pint wax milk cartons have been successfully used as containers. Cardboard soda bottle containers and discarded glass tumbler carry-alls have been commandeered as carrying cases. The half-pint milk carton can be re-sealed with a section of plastic notebook binder thus preventing the paint from drying between sessions.

Children can help in the preparation of tempera paint, mixing the various hues, tints, and shades and filling the individual paint containers to two-thirds capacity. For a class of 30 children about 60 containers of differents colors should be prepared. At least six white and four black paint containers should be available. All paints should be placed on a table or cart that is accessible from all sides and low enough so that the various colors are visible. There should be a fairly large watercolor brush for each color or container. Children take turns to choose the initial color they wish and a brush to paint with. When they are through with a color, they return the container with the brush in it to the supply table or cart. In this situation, it is recommended that the children painting use one color container at a time. In group situations they may have several colors at their table to share.

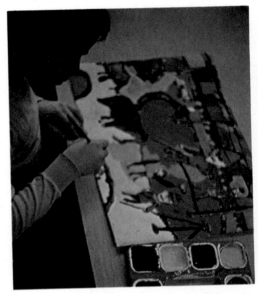

New strategies in the preparation, use, and storage of tempera paint have extended its use in schools. TOP—Discarded milk cartons fastened with clips or clothespins keep paint moist. CENTER—Tempera in tubs or cakes provide each child with his own palette and are easy to store. BOTTOM—"Autumn Trees." Grade 2, Athens, Georgia.

91

Adequate time should be allotted for clean-up procedures. Brushes, especially the kind with plastic handles and nonrusting ferrules, can be taken out of the paint containers, carefully squeezing or wiping off excess paint in the process, and placed in a large dishpan of soapy water to soak overnight. The next morning they can be rinsed and stored bristle-side up. Unless the paint in the baby food cans can be covered, the cans containing the paint should be stored in an air-tight cupboard or drawer. Some teachers have found clear plastic elasticized covers that keep paint moist in the cans. The dry paint that builds up on the inside and lip of the container should be scraped down into the container and diluted with water if necessary. Lips and edges of containers should be wiped clean with a damp cloth from time to time. Teachers have discovered that the excess paint does not build up as rapidly if a little liquid paraffin is applied to the container's edge or lip.

Semimoist cakes of opaque paint are now available in tubs or tins from several art supply sources and teachers who have used them recommend them mainly because of their time-saving clean-up and storage factors.

In the primary grades tempera painting is a natural for children. They take to it like ducks to water. The very young child especially enjoys making bold designs in paint and needs only an invitation to get started. Themes such as *Explosion in a Paint Factory, Fourth of July Fireworks, Butterflies in a Flower Garden,* and *Planets in Outer Space* can fire the youngster's imagination and his brush. Construction paper in assorted sizes and colors makes an excellent surface or ground for tempera paintings because the color of the paper can be utilized as part of the design if necessary. It also unifies the composition.

Children should be encouraged to compose their paintings whenever possible. A line drawing in white chalk or in brush and light colored paint rather than in pencil is recommended for the preliminary sketch. Other background papers for painting include white drawing, cream manila, gray manila, bogus, oatmeal, chipboard, corrugated board, wallpaper samples, brown wrapping, or classified sections of newspapers.

The following teaching strategies have proved helpful in tempera painting projects:

Put protective newspapers on the paint supply table and on individual painting areas.

Have a few moist cloths available for accidental paint spills. (Terry cloth remnants are recommended.)

Young children may wear old shirts as painting smocks.

Encourage children to repeat the color they are currently using in another part of their painting. This prevents excessive traffic to and from the supply table.

Remind children to wipe the excess paint off their brush against the lip of the container.

The figure, self-portrait or a friend, provides a natural stimulus for tempera painting as the illustrations on the opposite page show. The young boys in the third grade depicted themselves in favorite activities including fishing and hunt- *ing; the fourth-grade girls chose to paint themselves playing a musical instrument. Another group of fourth graders influenced by a circus then in town captured the clowns in all their color. Iowa City, Iowa.*

93

Caution them to be careful when painting next to a newly painted area because the two colors may run together.

Suggest that they wait until a color is thoroughly dry before painting over it to make a color change.

If brushes must be cleaned during the painting period, remind the students to squeeze out the excess water into the sink or the paint in the containers will eventually become diluted.

Storage of paintings should be supervised by the teacher so that wet paintings are not put on top of one another. They may be placed on the floor around the classroom or left on the desks if a recess or lunch period follows.

In the upper elementary grades children can exploit the various and complex possibilities of tempera painting because of their developing technical ability to control the paint and brush. They may design with paint on moist, colored, construction paper; utilize the dry-brush method to achieve texture; explore the mixed-media processes of tempera and crayon, tempera and India ink, tempera and yarn; or try painting on unusual surfaces or materials such as burlap, corrugated board, or papier-mâché.

Older children can be encouraged to mix a greater variety of tints, shades, or neutralized hues than are already available in the containers. They can use discarded pie tins or aluminum food trays for this purpose. They should be cautioned, however, not to mix more paint than they need. The substitute paint palettes should be rinsed out at the close of the period.

It is important to remember that growing youngsters cannot rush through a tempera painting project any more than they can rush through any qualitative endeavor. Sufficient time should be allotted for all phases of the project: preliminary sketching, making deliberate and sensitive color choices, developing contrast, pattern and detail, evaluating the final stages, and exhibiting the completed paintings.

Tempera painting should be included in every elementary art program because it expands and enriches the child's world of color and color relationships.

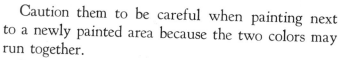

ABOVE LEFT—"The Three Kings." Grade 1. Oshkosh, Wisconsin. OPPOSITE PAGE—There is nothing quite like free flowing tempera or poster paint in its variety of colors to build the enthusiasm of the young child in art. LEFT and RIGHT—Grade 1. CENTER—Grade 3. Campus Elementary School, University of Wisconsin at Oshkosh.

95

96

TEMPERA BATIK

For upper elementary children who have had many experiences in tempera painting, the tempera batik process, which combines liquid tempera painting and India ink overpainting, is an exciting and challenging means of expression. The project, however, requires preplanning, effective materials organization, and a generous time allotment for the various steps of the process.

Almost any subject or motif can be interpreted in this medium, including figure composition, portraits, still life, and the various forms of flora and fauna. The batik project is similar in many respects to tempera painting but certain departures from basic tempera practices are necessary.

Liquid tempera, rather than powder or cake, is recommended.

The tempera should be of a rather creamy consistency; if too thin, the black ink will permeate it to neutralize the colors.

Bright colors and hues are often preferable to the dark browns, purples, and blues. Add a little white tempera to the darkest colors for best effects. Colors of high intensity add excitement and provide emphasis.

OPPOSITE PAGE—Tempera batik. Grade 5, Oshkosh, Wisconsin. TOP—Painting with tempera and allowing paper spaces between colors. CENTER—Completed painting before inking. BOTTOM—Tempera batik after coating with India ink and rinsing.

97

A sturdy paper should be used for the painting surface since the technique requires a final sponging or rinse-off process. Recommended background papers are construction paper in colors of light green, orange, pink, light blue, gray, and yellow, and heavy bogus or oatmeal paper. Do not use thin manila or tag.

Make the preliminary sketch in white chalk. Encourage the students to vary the pressure of the chalk line as they sketch so it will fluctuate from thick to thin. This will be an important consideration in the second phase, where the ink flows into the chalk lines.

As students paint, suggest that they paint up to, but not over, the chalk lines. The more varied the chalk lines or the paper surface remaining between two painted areas is, the more successful the composition will be.

Remind the youngsters not to paint those areas, shapes, or details that they wish to be solid black in the completed composition.

Remind the students also that a tempera color painted over another dry tempera color will wash off in the final rinsing process; that is why it is so important to plan colors before painting. However, tempera paint applied over wet tempera will not rinse off.

These tempera batiks are by youngsters in grades 5 and 6. Preliminary sketches were made at a natural museum.

98

Encourage the children to be inventive in their use of colors, to be daring, to be different. Guide them to mix many blues for a sky, many greens for grass, many hues for flowers.

Unpainted spaces may be left between objects, between objects and background, in patterned areas between dots or stripes of color, and wherever areas of black are needed for contrasting effects.

For example, the interstices between fern fronds, bird feathers, fish scales, and tree bark left unpainted will permit the black ink coat to flow into these spaces and create an exciting contrast of color against black.

When all the desired colored areas are painted, the work should be stored or shelved to dry completely.

When the painting is completely dry, a coat of waterproof black India ink, undiluted or slightly diluted with water, is applied. Use a soft bristle utility brush, 1 or 2 inches wide, and apply the ink in an even coat. Be generous with the ink; load the brush. Do not exert too much pressure on the brush.

Allow the ink coat to dry thoroughly before the final rinse or wash. The length of the drying period may vary from a few hours to an overnight period, depending on humidity and the season. Do not rinse or spray too soon.

TOP—"A Flower Garden." Grade 6, Atlanta, Georgia. CENTER and BOTTOM—"County Fair." Grades 4 and 5, Athens, Georgia.

99

For the final washing or rinsing process put the painting on a sheet of masonite, discarded cafe or cookie tin, slightly larger than the painting, and wash off the ink using water from spray or faucet. In mild weather the paintings may be taken outside and rinsed off with a water hose. Be sure the paintings are always on a board during the wash because if handled when wet they tear very easily.

It is best to begin the rinse in the center of the painting and then wash outwards. Do not direct water to one spot too long unless the ink adheres too strongly.

Sometimes a wet sponge or a finger rub can be used to bring out the color in an area where the ink sticks too rigidly.

When the washing and rinsing process is completed (a final clean rinse is important), use unfolded paper towels or newspapers to blot the painting.

While the paintings are moist, they may be retouched to correct washed-out areas but this should be done carefully to approximate the blurred edges of the batik process. When dry, oil pastels may be used for retouching. When thoroughly dry, the batiks may be given a coat of clear shellac, clear polymer, or liquid wax to enrich the colors and protect the surface.

100

TOP—Grade 3, Iowa City, Iowa. BOTTOM—Rinsing off the India ink coating. This may be done also with a spray attachment at the sink. Allow the ink to dry a few hours or overnight before rinsing. OPPOSITE PAGE—Self-portraits. Tempera batik. Grade 1, Iowa City, Iowa.

 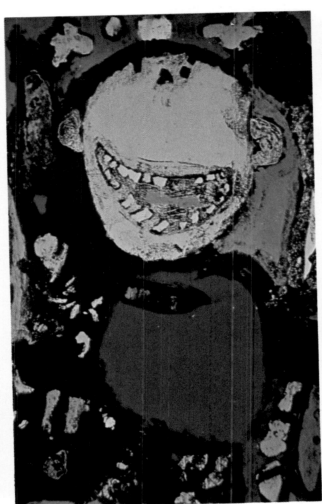 

MAKING A MURAL

If the planning and making of a group mural is to be a valid and worthwhile art experience for the youngsters, the aesthetic requirements of mural art should be considered as carefully as possible or the effort made by the children may dissipate into a haphazard or unresolved performance.

Initially, the students and the teacher must decide whether the project, technique, or subject matter is adaptable to a mural undertaking. Certain themes are more appropriate and more stimulating for group mural endeavors because of their complexity or because of their appeal to a certain age group. For very young children the following mural topics are suggested: *A Bird Sanctuary, Land of Make-Believe, Fish in the Sea, Noah's Ark, A Flower Garden, On the Farm, Animals in the Jungle or Zoo, Summer Games.* Older children will respond to the following themes: *Fun at the Beach, Astronauts in Space, Aquanauts on the Ocean Floor, The Rodeo, State Fair, Rock Festival, The Big Parade, From Wheels to Jets: A History of Transportation, Kite Contest, Three-Ring Circus, Playground Fun, Winter Carnival, Block Party, Shopping Mall,* and *Track Meet.*

102

Before the children begin a mural the teacher might ask the following questions: "What is a mural? Why do artists paint murals? Who made the first murals? Are there any murals in our city, county, or state?" More specifically, the teacher might pose the following queries: "What theme should be used for the mural? What techniques or medium should be employed? How large should the mural be? Where can we work on it? Where could the mural be displayed when completed? How shall each student's contribution to the mural be decided?"

When all the youngsters have finished their contributions to the mural and all the individual pieces are tentatively pinned or stapled to the background, the students, with teacher guidance, should devote at least one class period to composing the mural. Here the teacher's tact and gentle persuasion are most important. It should be brought to the attention of the children that a mural is somewhat like a giant painting and consequently demands similar compositional consideration. Look for varied sizes of objects or figures, varied heights, varied break-up of space in foreground and background, overlapping of shapes, avenues leading into the picture, grouping of objects or figures or animals for unity, quiet areas to balance the busy or complex ones, larger figures or objects at bottom and smaller ones higher up in order to create an illusion of distance or space.

Inevitably, there will be the delicate dilemma where one child's contribution overlaps that of another.

ABOVE and OPPOSITE PAGE—Group mural by children in summer art class. Theme: "Fun in the Park." A primer coat of oil paint was applied to a 10′ x 200′ plywood barrier. The linear composition based on sketches made in the city park was made in black enamel with 1-inch-wide utility brushes. The colors (leftovers of enamel paint donated by parents) were then applied, painting up to, but not over, the black enamel outlines. Grades 1 through 6, Iowa City, Iowa. Mural now in collection of Smithsonian Institution, Washington, D.C.

Here the teacher can wisely smooth troubled waters by pointing out that overlapping shapes create unity and the children can take turns overlapping their figures if they wish. When the separate pieces are finally arranged in a composition that is satisfying, exciting, and colorful, they may be more permanently pinned or stapled down. If the mural is mounted on a separate sheet of Upsonboard or heavy cardboard, it may be displayed in the school's entrance foyer or in the lunch room for all the children to enjoy.

For example, if *Fun on the Playground* is selected as the subject of the mural and cut and pasted paper as the medium, the following questions might be asked: "How many different kinds of games and sports should be included? Let's make a list on the chalkboard. How shall we decide which game each student will select to portray? How many different areas of the playground will be shown? What pieces of playground equipment should we include? Should all the children on the playground be the same size?

ABOVE—Group mural. Grade 4. Theme: "Winter Fun." The individual figures, trees, houses, and birds were colored with oil crayon on manila paper, cut out, arranged, and stapled to a 4' x 8' corkboard on which white paper and blue-colored tissue paper had been applied beforehand.

More approaches in making group murals. TOP LEFT—Class portrait. Arms outstretched, happy smiles on their bright faces, the first graders face life with high hopes! TOP RIGHT—Everbody pitches in! Dad's shirt comes in handy as a painting smock. BOTTOM—"Our Community Helpers." Today they include astronauts as well as aquanauts. Grades 4 and 5. Athens, Georgia.

ABOVE—Japanese school children paint a mural directly, freely, expressively. The theme: "A World of Transportation." Note the functional tempera container. BELOW LEFT—Youngsters crayoning imaginative fish which they will suspend in mobile fashion much like the tempera-painted two-sided fish in illustration right which were stuffed with newspapers and stapled together.

Will they all be dressed alike? What patterns might we see in their clothes? What kind of day will it be? Cloudy? Windy? Rainy? What else could you incorporate in your playground mural? What about trees, bushes, goalposts, fences, dogs, birds, drinking fountains, nets, balls, bats, mitts, signs?"

Various media and techniques can be employed in making murals. For free, expressive murals that are painted directly on a background surface such as oaktag, wrapping paper, cardboard, or construction paper, use tempera, enamel, latex, or acrylic paints. For murals that are assembled after the children have completed separately assigned parts, use cut colored construction paper, cloth remnants, magazine ads, yarn, chalk, crayon, oil pastel, colored tissue, and *found materials*.

In the pin-up, staple-on type of mural, the children tentatively pin their completed contributions to a selected background. This may be corkboard, Celotex, colored display paper (plain or corrugated), wallboard, burlap, or a large sheet of cardboard painted appropriately. Children who complete their contributions early may be assigned other parts to enhance the composition. Depending on the subject of the mural, these additional embellishments might include trees, flowers, bushes, houses, fences, rocks, stars, kites, snowflakes, clouds, insects, birds, spiderwebs, planes, sun, moon, rockets, or telephone poles.

TOP—Individual contributions create a space traffic jam of the future. Grades 3 and 4. CENTER—Cloth remnants provide the unique effects for this beautiful collage mural. Grade 6, Pinellas County Schools, Florida. BOTTOM— This colorful group mural in cut colored construction paper enlivens a whole cafeteria wall.

107

CRAYON

The wax crayon in assorted colors has been a standard and widely accepted art medium in the elementary schools for over half a century. More recently, resourceful teachers have combined it with other media to provide variety and renewed interest in their art programs. A number of these innovative techniques, including crayon resist, crayon engraving, and multicrayon engraving, are described in detail on the following pages.

However, the varied and rich potential of wax crayon by itself with its own singular merits has not always been fully investigated and exploited. The ordinary classroom projects in crayon are usually weak in color intensity, in value contrasts, and in textural quality. Crayon is employed too often as a pallid, sketchy coloring medium instead of the glowing, vibrant, and vitally expressive pigmentation it can be. It is very important that the rich possibilities of the crayon be identified and explored from the first grade on if children are expected to grow in crayoning skills.

At every grade level, a class session of manipulation and experimentation with the multicolored crayons is recommended. Whenever possible, recommend that the youngsters or the school obtain the large 64-color crayon box with its beautiful range of tints and shades as well as its wide selection of neutralized hues. To help the children achieve the most qualitative results, the teacher may have to prompt the youngsters to apply the crayon with a heavier pressure to bring out the richest colors; to employ newspaper padding when they crayon; to point out the excitement of contrasting colors; to challenge the youngsters to create color patterns of stripes, plaids, and dots; and to stress the utilization of seldom employed colors such as ochre, umber, sienna, black, gray, and white. Older children can be encouraged to investigate the varied applications of crayon over crayon.

The whole mood of a crayon composition changes when color is applied to varicolored or varitextured surfaces. Have the children work on a background

OPPOSITE PAGE—A live cat and kittens brought to class provided the visual inspiration for this crayon painting. The composition was sketched in a light crayon on colored construction paper. The color crayons were then applied richly and imaginatively in the next two art sessions.

other than the commonly used manila or white drawing paper. Suggest the utilization of colored construction paper as a crayon surface. Student and teacher alike will be surprised and elated by the possibilities of vibrant crayon on pink, red-orange, brown, purple, blue-green, and yellow-green construction paper. If the children are encouraged to permit areas of the construction paper to show, especially between objects, they will see eventually how the background-paper color can unify their compositions. Suggest that the youngsters try their crayons first on the back of the colored sheet to see how the color of the paper subtly changes the color of the applied crayon.

Preliminary sketches for crayon pictures should be made with a white or very light-colored crayon (or white chalk) rather than with pencil. This will minimize the frustration children experience when they attempt to use a blunt crayon to color the minute details of a pencil sketch.

Encourage the children to use the crayon boldly and to color the objects or shapes from the inside out rather than outlining every object first. Suggest that colors be repeated to achieve unity. Completed crayon compositions may be given a glowing surface sheen by burnishing or rubbing them with a folded paper towel or tissue.

The most recurring problem the teacher of art faces is the case of the child who rushes through his crayoning or who quickly colors in one or two shapes and insists he is finished. There are no sure-fire remedies for dilemmas such as these but certainly one of the most successful strategies for insuring a happy outcome in crayon projects is a teacher's well-planned visual motivation that leads to a richly developed preliminary drawing which in turn provides the springboard for rich crayoning.

Cats and their kittens usually provide interesting subject matter for children's drawings and paintings. TOP LEFT— An imaginative treatment of a cat family at home. Note that they own a human to play with. Oshkosh, Wisconsin.

OPPOSITE PAGE—A rainy day inspired this composition. Youngsters took turns modeling in raincoats and umbrellas, then created expressive patterns for their clothes and backgrounds. Crayon. Grade 4.

The crayon-watercolor resist painting has always held a certain magic for youngsters of all ages. To be successful, however, the children must be guided to apply the crayons with enough pressure so the wax will resist the watercolor. White drawing or construction paper is best for the surface. Use a light crayon rather than pencil for the preliminary drawing.

CRAYON RESIST

The combination of the glowing wax crayon and wet, flowing watercolor on white drawing or construction paper provides an exciting creative experience for children of all ages. Subject matter themes which are rich in pattern and texture, such as fish, birds, flowers, and reptiles, are highly recommended for this technique. The insect world especially provides a wealth of inspiration for crayon resist projects. Youngsters are often excited by the variety of insects found in their environment and the teacher can stimulate further participation by encouraging them to collect specimens and share them with their classmates. Other sources, such as illustrated books, color slides, and films on insects, will aid in broadening the child's awareness of insect life and give him a richer understanding of its limitless variety.

A study of the insect world helps the child in art because in the structure of almost every insect he finds various aspects and components of design such as the filigree pattern of a butterfly's, dragonfly's, or moth's wings, the rhythmic segments of a grasshopper's abdomen, the contrasting motifs on a cicada's back, the simplicity of the symmetrical balance of a ladybug's body, or the curvilinear grace of a praying mantis' legs.

TOP—Fish in an aquarium or in the sea is a particularly suitable theme for crayon resist. Grade 6, Rangoon, Burma. CENTER—Flowers and insects lend themselves beautifully to crayon resist paintings. Nine different approaches from Iowa City, Iowa, Grade 3. Bottom—"A Rainy Day." Rain drops make wonderful patterns. Grade 4, Athens, Georgia.

113

In the crayon-resist technique, the patterns and designs of the subject chosen are most important. The different species and sizes of the insects will often guarantee variety in the composition. Usually the more insects the child incorporates in his crayon composition, the richer and more complex the design becomes and, subsequently, the negative areas evolve into exciting and unique shapes. The environmental aspects lead to overall unity. Background flowers, weeds, grasses, trees, branches, rock formations, webs, vines, pollen, sun, and clouds all help tie the composition together.

A successful crayon-resist painting depends on the following technical requirements: the crayon must be applied to the white drawing or construction paper with a heavy pressure so that the crayon surface will resist the watercolor or tempera paint that is applied in the final stage of the process. A good way to insure a solid application of crayon is to utilize several layers of newspaper padding under the paper when crayoning. In order to capitalize on the full effect of this medium, the student should plan to leave certain areas of the paper uncrayoned, for example, between two objects, between two colors, and between object and background, as well as sections within shapes or objects, such as veins within leaves or wings.

114

Stages in a crayon resist painting. TOP—Classmates provided the visual motivation. CENTER—The crayon composition emphasizing exploitation of pattern, texture, and rich application of crayon. BOTTOM—The completed work after application of rich watercolor in bright segments.

Encourage the youngsters to be imaginative in their employment of the color crayons. White crayon can be especially effective in this technique but on white paper it is difficult to distinguish. Black crayon provides strong contrast; however, if a black tempera final wash is planned, black crayon should not be used.

When the crayoning is completed, two techniques of resist may be employed—the wet process or the dry process. In the dry method, the student paints directly over his crayon composition using water-color or water-diluted tempera. If the crayon has not been applied heavily enough, the paint will sometimes obliterate the crayon, but in some instances this situation can be partially corrected by quickly running water over the paper to remove the excess paint. It is highly recommended that the teacher test the viscosity of the tempera paint on a sample crayoned sheet before allowing the children to go ahead with the final painting stage.

In the wet method the desks or tables of a painting area should be covered with newspapers. The children immerse their crayoned papers in water until it is thoroughly wet, then carry it to their desks or painting table. They then load their brushes with watercolor and drop or float the color on the white areas of the paper. They may also let the brush trail

Crayon resist paintings are ideal in situations where time is too limited to produce rich in-depth crayon paintings. If a 50-minute period is devoted to the crayoning, the water-color painting can often be completed in another art period of similar length.

around the edges of the crayoned objects and let the paint flow to the center. They may use one color for unity or a variety of colors for excitement. The wet process is especially recommended for resist compositions dealing with undersea or aquarium themes. Sometimes white areas of the paper left unpainted can be very effective. For a large class the teacher might prepare beforehand several containers of water-diluted tempera or watercolor in assorted hues. A large table or a counter space near a sink could be designated as an area for applying the paint over the crayon compositions.

When applying watercolor washes in crayon-resist projects, the teacher and students must remember that the watercolor always looks twice as dark when it is wet. When it dries its brilliancy often diminishes, so students must be instructed to apply it richly. Sometimes a second coat of watercolor is advisable.

In addition to the colorful world of insects, the following subjects are recommended for crayon-resist paintings: *A Flower Garden, Fireworks Display, The Circus, The Fair, Halloween Parade, Imaginative Designs, Fruit and Vegetable Still Life.*

Fair and carnival themes are sometimes popular as crayon resist subject matter. The colorful stands and rides open up many decorative and imaginative possibilities. Grade 6, Oshkosh, Wisconsin. OPPOSITE PAGE—A simple linear approach in resist painting. White crayon applied to cream manila paper, then coated with black tempera paint. Crayon must be applied heavily. Grade 2.

CRAYON ENCAUSTIC

Actually, crayon encaustic may be too pretentious a name for the simple, though exciting, melted-crayon technique described in this chapter but it does have a family relationship. The encaustic process may be the kind of art adventure that reserved only for those upper elementary teachers and their young charges who are brave in heart, eager to try something new, and patient enough to salvage a year's supply of broken crayons.

What this project demands more than anything else is a surplus of discarded crayons in all colors and all sized pieces. One enthusiastic classroom teacher makes the encaustic painting activity an annual spring event which the children look forward to with great anticipation. Naturally, because the crayons are used throughout the year, this project must be a school year's-end affair.

Remove paper wrapping from the accumulated crayons, break into small pieces, and place in baby food jars or small juice tins. Each jar or tin should contain crayons of a different color. Because of space limitations the number of different color jars may have to be curtailed. However, the basic colors plus white, black, pink, turquoise, magenta, chartreuse, ochre, gray, brown, and tints of blue, green, and purple should be made available.

OPPOSITE PAGE—These beautiful paintings were made employing the melted crayon or encaustic process. Size 9" x 12". A bowl of blossoming anemones provided the visual inspiration. Color reproductions of flower paintings by noted artists such as Odilon Redon, Vincent VanGogh, and Paul Gauguin were displayed and discussed.

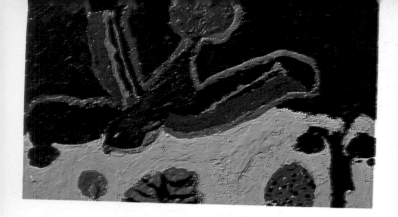

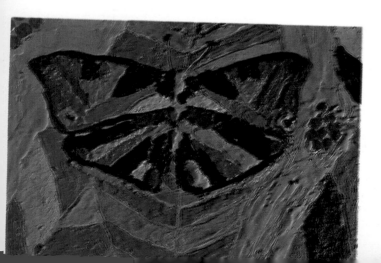

The most functional working station for an encaustic-painting project is a large newspaper-protected table. If available, find a table somewhat lower in height than the ordinary reading table. Place an electric hot plate in the middle of this table. If necessary, two plates may be used or a plate with two burners. Use a long electric extension cord so that there is working space between electric outlet and the table.

Put the crayon-filled jars or tins in a discarded (2 to 2½ inches deep) baking pan. Fill the pan generously with water and place on the hot plate. Turn on electric current. When crayons have melted, put one or more Q-tips or small watercolor brushes in each container. These should be old brushes, if possible, that can be designated for this project only.

If the hot water in the pan is kept at the level of the melted crayon in the jars or tins, the crayon will keep a flowing painting consistency.

Do not crowd the working area. A group of four to six students, depending on the size of the table, is recommended.

A preliminary sketch for a crayon encaustic painting is usually recommended. A flower bouquet, an exotic bird in foliage, a fantastic fish in seaweed, or a clown's face are subject matter possibilities.

120

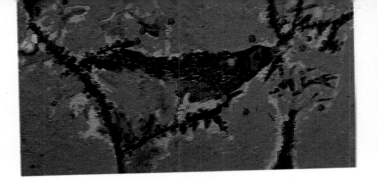

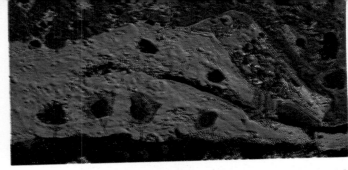

A medium weight white cardboard approximately 9 by 12, 12 by 12, or 12 by 16 inches is recommended as the painting surface. Scrap mat board, chipboard, or grocery carton board coated with white latex paint are other suggested surfaces.

The teacher must supervise the encaustic painting process rather carefully. The water must not be allowed to boil out in the pan. The current must be regulated from time to time so the melted crayon does not cool off. Crayon brushes or applicators should not be switched from container to container.

Children should take turns with the color they need.

This is a project that cannot be rushed. Sometimes the beauty of the encaustic does not materialize until after several layers of crayon have overlapped. There will be an exciting impasto quality to the finished work if time is taken. If one color is applied over another, there is the possibility of further embellishment by incising lines with a nail to reveal the color underneath. It is a project full of surprises with a color richness that is unsurpassed. Be brave and try it!

OPPOSITE PAGE and ABOVE—Crayon encaustic paintings. Grade 5, Lawton Elementary School, Ann Arbor, Michigan. Powdered tempera and melted beeswax may be mixed to supplement the crayon supply.

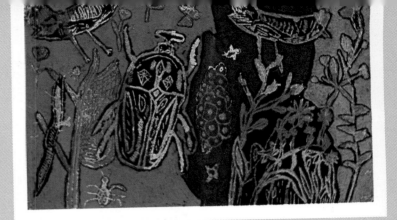

CRAYON ENGRAVING

Crayon engraving, a technique involving the use of crayon and black poster paint, has become a popular and standard project in many elementary schools, but its many exciting and varied possibilities have not yet been fully explored. Students are too often satisfied with quick, superficial designs or with hasty, random scribbles and scratches. New worlds of pattern and texture are still to be discovered and the combination of crayon engraving with other media, such as oil pastel, to enhance the process invites further exploration.

Basically, the crayon-engraving technique employs a linear approach. Therefore subject matter or compositions which are rich in line, texture, and pattern are best suited to this medium. Students can turn, for instance, to the natural world for their inspiration; to animals like the porcupine, anteater, armadillo, zebra; to birds, especially those of exotic plummage; to reptiles such as turtles, iguanas, and horned toads; to insects such as dragonflies, praying mantes, butterflies, and beetles; to crustaceans such as crabs and crayfish; to fish of any species; indeed to all varieties of plant life.

OPPOSITE PAGE—The insect world comes alive in the expressive creation of an observant child. The crayon engraving process embellished in the final stages with oil pastel has a richness and glow unmatched. Grade 4, Madison County, Georgia. RIGHT—A fourth-grade teacher introduced color photographs and color slides of insects to inspire her students. Athens, Georgia.

123

The preliminary drawing for a crayon engraving should be made in pencil on newsprint or thin manila paper of the same size as the desired final composition. This will prove helpful especially if the student decides to transfer his drawing as suggested in the process.

The first step in this technique is to apply varied colors of crayon to a selected paper surface. Recommended papers for this background are white drawing, white construction, or oak tag. The application of the crayon can take several forms, but in each case it should be applied evenly and with strong pressure so that the paper surface is completely covered. Several layers of newspaper employed as padding during the crayoning will help insure an even, rich coating of crayon. The youngster may begin in the crayoning phase by first making a scribble design in a light-colored crayon and then filling in the scribbled shapes solidly with a variety of bright colors; he may apply rich swatches or patches of color that slightly overlap; or he can relate his color areas to coincide with his drawing. A limited or full color range can be employed for the crayon background depending upon the mood or effect desired. In any case the brightest and darkest colors are recommended for the best effects. Black crayon should not be applied.

After the crayoning has been completed and the surface crayon flecks are brushed or wiped off with a paper towel, a tempera coating is applied. In most cases, black tempera has been recommended but other possibilities are brown, red, white, blue, green, or

---

124

Steps in crayon engraving. TOP—Youngsters apply the crayon. Paper size can range from 9″ x 12″ to 18″ x 24″ depending on age and time scheduled for art. CENTER— Engraving line and pattern through the black paint. BOT- TOM—Applying final embellishment with oil pastel.

purple. The tempera paint, either liquid or powdered (mixed with water), should be of a milky creamy consistency. To make it adhere to the waxy crayoned surface, it must be mixed with a very small amount of liquid soap, approximately a tablespoonful to a pint of tempera.

When the tempera coated surface is thoroughly dry, the student may transfer his sketch or preliminary line drawing by coating the reverse side of it with white crayon, then placing it (white-crayoned surface down) on the black tempera-coated side and with pencil or ball-point tip making the transfer. There is also available on the market a white or yellow dressmaker's carbon paper which is recommended highly for the transfer of any drawing to a dark surface.

The next step is the actual engraving or incising through the tempera to the crayon. A preliminary outline engraving with a nail, compass point, or scratch pen is suggested. Be sure the students place newspapers under their work because the engraving can be a slightly messy process.

After a linear composition is achieved, the youngster can delineate the textural or patterned areas using a variety of tools, including pins, broken combs, or metal nail files. High contrast can be achieved by scraping away some areas down to the surface of the crayon with paring knife, scratch pen, or single-edge razor blades.

After the student has completed the engraving processes, he may enrich his composition by superimposing the new oil pastel colors over some of the black tempera surfaces or the engraved surfaces. Finally, the entire composition may be enhanced in many instances by engraving patterns and textures through the pasteled areas.

Crayon engraving is a fascinating mixed-media technique that opens new avenues to color, pattern, and texture discoveries, especially for the upper-grade youngster.

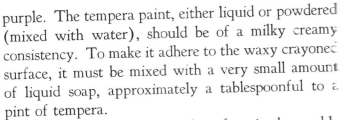

The visual inspiration and the resulting engraving. Note rich delineation of pattern and texture. Grade 6.

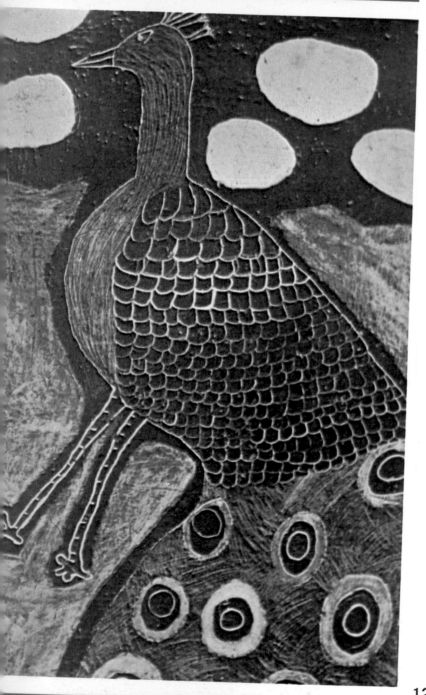

MULTICRAYON ENGRAVING

An engraving project that offers special opportunities for unusual color-glazing effects is the multi-crayon-over-crayon engraving. This is basically an intaglio technique that relies on an exploitation of incised lines, patterns, and textures as the major compositional elements. Multicrayon engraving can be included in the elementary school's art repertoire from the first grade on.

For this process, wax crayons and a strong paper with a smooth or shiny surface are required. Suggested papers include tagboard, railroad or poster board in assorted colors, or fingerpaint paper. A generous amount of newspaper padding should be employed during the crayoning process. All the color crayons can be used, but it is recommended that a partially limited color sequence be planned.

Children can make their own unique holiday greeting cards by using the blank side of a postcard to create their multi-crayon engraving designs. The size and surface of a postcard lends itself beautifully to this technique.

It is advisable to begin with a solid, even coat of a light crayon such as yellow, pink, light green, or blue because a dark initial crayon coat stains the surface of the paper making it difficult to distinguish the engraved lines. Successive layers of crayon should be applied over the first light-colored coating, building from light to dark and back to light as desired. Apply the crayon in short, swift strokes with a definite pressure. You may change the direction of the strokes for better coverage. However, do not exert too much pressure on the crayon, since this tends to damage previous layers. White crayon over a black or a dark crayon coat creates unusual color effects. If too stark, this white crayon coating may be altered by applying tints of light green, blue, or red crayon. A facial tissue or paper towel may be used to burnish the completed crayoned surface before beginning the engraving process.

If a preliminary sketch has been made (a procedure which is highly recommended), the students may use one of two methods to utilize this sketch. They may use the sketch as inspiration (referring to it as they engrave directly on the crayoned surface) or they may transfer the sketch to the crayon surface as a guide for engraving. This is done by coating the reverse side of the sketch with black or white crayon, placing it over the multicrayoned surface (crayoned sides touching), and going over the lines with a pencil

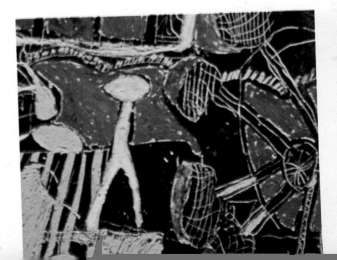

More multicrayon interpretations. TOP and BOTTOM— Theme: "The Carnival." Grade 4, Ann Arbor, Michigan. Color slides were employed as visual stimulus. CENTER —"My Pet." Grade 1.

127

or ball-point pen. If the multicrayon final surface is relatively dark, use a white crayon to coat back of sketch before transfer; if the surface is white or light colored, use a black crayon to coat back of sketch to be transferred. The direct engraving often has an immediacy and spontaneity that is refreshing, but thoughtless, haphazard scratching of the surface should be discouraged.

Tools found to be most effective for the engraving process include nails, metal nail files, pointed dowel sticks, scissor points, wooden ceramic tools, compass points, plastic picnic and paring knives. Discarded dental tools and nut picks will also come in handy. The commercial Sloyd or Hyde knife, which is a pointed knife with a curved 2-inch blade that is blunt enough to be safe, produces either a thin to heavy line and can scrape away a whole surface when necessary. This knife is highly recommended for a number of projects, including sculpture.

For children in the primary grades a small-sized crayoning surface is recommended. Use either fingerpaint paper, oak tag, or colored railroad board in about 9 by 12 or 12 by 12 inch pieces. Fingerpaint paper should be reinforced on the back edges with masking tape. The crayon application is time consuming and young children have a limited working span. However, they tackle the technique with enthusiasm and the color combinations they produce are unique and evocative. The teacher should not limit them in the variety of colors they use. The crayon overlays may range from yellow to orange to red to purple to black and back to white again. There should be a clear demonstration, however, of the best way to apply the crayon for richest effects.

In the intermediate or upper grades, larger sheets of fingerpaint paper, oak tag, or colored railroad board (12 by 18 or 18 by 18 inches) may be introduced. Students may experiment with the crayons on the back of the paper at first to see the effects of color on color.

Multicrayon engravings on plain oak tag or fingerpaint paper may be embellished further by staining or glazing with acrylic or polymer colors in tints of umber, sepia, sienna, ochre, and earth green. With a soft, water-moistened cloth, rub the paint over the engraved surface and wipe off the excess. Be sure the paint stains the incised lines. One acrylic color, such as raw umber, may be rubbed over the entire surface to unify the composition or a variety of colors may be exploited for a more exciting effect. *Caution:* Use the paint diluted as a glaze or stain only. Do not apply as a solid opaque covering.

With the introduction of bright colored poster, railroad, and day-glo color boards as surfaces for multicrayon engraving, the final staining or glazing step is no longer necessary since the color of the board itself, seen through the engraved crayon, adds a rich complementary effect of its own.

Multicrayon engraving adds an exciting dimension to the potential of the common crayon. It opens up a whole new world of color discoveries for the elementary school youngster. Try it!

OPPOSITE PAGE—Multicrayon engraving, "Pets and Friends." Grade 1, Lakewood Elementary School, Ann Arbor, Michigan.

130

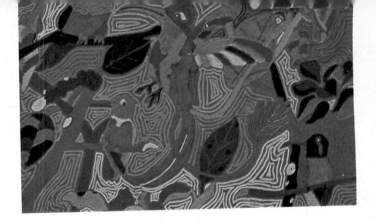

OIL PASTEL

The relatively new oil pastels now on the art market have opened up a whole new world of color expression in the elementary art program. They come in a wide range of hues and are certainly within the budget range of most schools. Their most attractive feature is the ease with which the young children can apply them to obtain rich, vibrant colors. Their only drawback, if any, is that they have a tendency to stain, so youngsters should be cautioned to protect their clothes when they use pastels.

Colored construction paper is highly recommended as a background surface for oil pastel paintings. In many cases a preliminary sketch in white chalk or light pastel is suggested.

OPPOSITE PAGE—A glowing composition in oil pastel on colored construction paper. Illustrations on this page show the painting in its developmental stages. Grade 6, Athens, Georgia.

Children should be encouraged to use the pastel colors boldly and imaginatively, pressing hard to achieve the richest, most vibrant effects. They should be guided to color objects or shapes from the inside out rather than outlining a shape in one color and coloring it another. They should be challenged to repeat colors, to use white, gray, and black as contrasting effects, and instructed to exploit the background paper color, letting it show between pasteled areas to achieve unity.

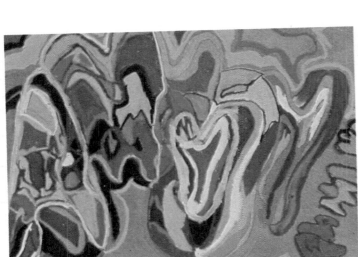

OPPOSITE PAGE. TOP LEFT—"A Beautiful Garden." Grade 1. TOP RIGHT—"A Snowstorm." Grade 2. BOTTOM RIGHT—"Butterflies in the Garden." Grade 5. BOTTOM LEFT—"Our Feathered Friends." Grade 4, Birmingham, Alabama. THIS PAGE. LEFT, top to bottom—Students' names become part of a colorful design. These could be laminated for personal notebook covers. RIGHT, top to bottom—"Space Ships." Grades 4, 5, and 6. Grades 3 and 4, Barnett Shoals Elementary School, Athens, Georgia.

OIL PASTEL RESIST

Teachers familiar with crayon resist techniques will welcome oil pastel as a resist medium because it does not require the high consumption of time and the intense exertion on the part of the children that the successful application of crayon demands.

Basically the same steps as crayon resist are followed. A preliminary drawing can be made on either white or colored construction paper (in yellow or white chalk). The pastel is applied with definite pressure so it will resist the final coat of paint. Areas of paper are left showing between pasteled areas, between objects or figures, between objects or figures and background, between patterns and textures. White and gray pastel may be used. Black should be avoided since the final resist effect will be achieved with black paint.

OPPOSITE PAGE—Oil pastel resist. Inspiration was provided by introducing color photographs and color slides of insects, spiderwebs, and flowers. Illustrations at right on this page show steps in the technique. Grade 5, Barnett Shoals School, Athens, Georgia.

135

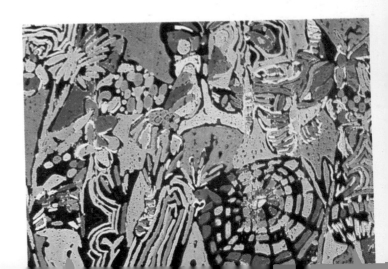

A youngster applies a coat of fairly thin black tempera or poster paint over his oil pastel composition. The paint fills in all the uncolored areas and creates a batik effect over the pasteled areas. OPPOSITE PAGE—Inspiration and expression. White oil pastel preliminary line drawing becomes part of the composition. Clarke and Madison County Schools, Georgia.

Evaluate the completed coloring for variety of colors, repetition of colors, repetition of pattern of texture, many varied open spaces of uncolored paper, and rich application of pastel.

Place the pastel composition on a newspaper-protected surface and apply a coat of fairly thin black tempera paint with a 1½-inch-wide soft bristle utility brush. Hold the loaded brush horizontally. Let it float on the surface. Try the paint first on a practice pastel-colored sheet of paper. If it covers the pastel, it is too thick. Dilute with water. Use a clean newspaper surface for each pastel resist painted.

Oil pastel resists have proven one of the most rewarding and exciting art techniques in the elementary school art program.

COLLAGE

One of the most exciting and popular forms of visual expression in elementary schools today is the art of collage.

A half century ago shock and dismay greeted the initial collages of Pablo Picasso, Georges Braque, Juan Gris, and Hans Arp. Today their creations in paste (the word collage derives from the French *coller*—to paste), paper, and other discards from the wastebasket appear relatively tame. The wellsprings from which current collagists draw their materials is so bountiful in content and variety that there are practically no limits to contemporary collage or assemblage expression.

There are many approaches to the art of collage. They range from simple cutting and pasting of colored paper or cloth to complex sewing or shearing and gluing of plastics, plywood, cardboard, and *found objects*. Some recommended materials for elementary collage are colored poster and construction paper, fluorescent and day-glo paper, cloth remnants, found materials, wallpaper and rug samples, multicolored tissue paper, colored sections and ads from magazines.

Collage utilizing cut and torn colored construction paper. Theme: "On Our Street." Size 18" x 24". Grade 1, Iowa City, Iowa.

Children of all ages enjoy cutting, tearing, and pasting, so teachers will find the collage project a most effective avenue for teaching the many elements of composition: variety of shapes, overlapping to create unity and subtle depth, positive and negative space concepts, color contrast and relationship, balance, pattern, and emphasis. The fact that the objects or shapes the youngster cuts out can be shifted or changed before he decides on the final arrangement gives him and the teacher a welcome opportunity to discuss the composition before he pastes or glues the separate pieces permanently.

Teachers will find many of the following suggestions useful in helping children with their collage expressions.

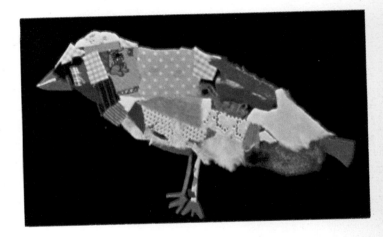

> Cut and arrange the big shapes of your composition first.
> If you are using a colored background, be sure to exploit it in your design. Let some of the color background show to help unify your composition.
> Try different materials for the background surface: chipboard, oak tag, plywood, burlap, discarded bamboo or straw placemats, corrugated board, railroad or poster board, wallpaper book samples.

TOP and BOTTOM—Cut construction paper pin-up mural and details. Each child contributed one animal. Grade 1, Barnett Shoals Schools, Athens, Georgia. CENTER—Cloth remnants collage. Grade 3, Japan. Note emphasis given to eye, beak, and claws.

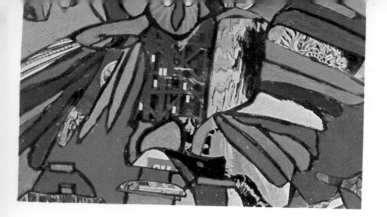

OPPOSITE PAGE. LEFT—*Cloth remnants combined with paint are exploited in these unique and delightful collages. Grade 4, Campus School, University of Wisconsin at Oshkosh. RIGHT—A variety of found materials provided exciting and continuous motivation for these collages. Preliminary sketches were first made at the site. Grade 6, Iowa City, Iowa.*

Small details or pattern can be pasted on the large shapes before the large shapes are adhered to the surface.

Overlapping of shapes can be exploited in the collage technique more successfully than in any other art form. As children mature, they can be guided to see the unusual shapes and the suggestion of depth they can create through overlapping.

Some eye-catching materials such as tinfoil, shiny plastic, and cellophane have a strong fascination for children and, if not cautioned, they are apt to use them in an unrestrained, haphazard manner. Suggest their utilization as elements of emphasis.

Repetition of a color, shape value, or pattern can help give unity to a collage; however, instead of repeating an element, say a color, in the same intensity or size, change it slightly when repeating it for variety.

Recommend the use of uneven rather than an even number of repeated elements; for example, repeat a certain shape or color three times rather than twice.

Encourage the use of informal rather than formal balance in collage compositions.

Avoid a lot of "sticky" problems by using a discarded magazine as a paste-applying surface. When the child needs a clean pasting area, he just turns to another page in the magazine.

(See Appendix E for a list of assorted materials useful in collage projects.)

A mounted owl brought to the class by the teacher became the visual impetus for these colorful collage mixed media creations. Grade 6, Barnett Shoals School, Athens, Georgia.

140

OPPOSITE PAGE. LEFT—Found materials provided part of the motivation for this collage project. The theme was "Self-portraits." Grade 4. Oshkosh, Wisconsin. RIGHT— Torn advertisements from old magazines provided the color for this unusual collage. A classmate posed with a guitar for the preliminary sketch. Grade 5, Danielsville, Georgia. ABOVE—A subject they can identify with often whets the student's interest in art. The motorcycle is definitely part of the youngster's everyday environment. Grade 6, Atlanta, Georgia.

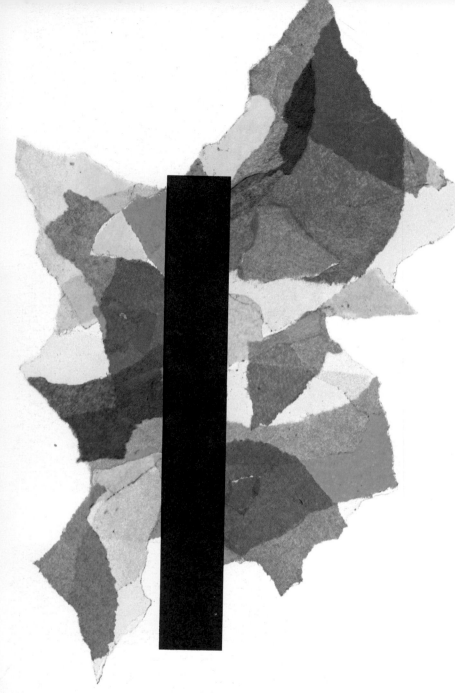

TISSUE PAPER COLLAGE

On the first day of a tissue-collage project the teacher might surprise the class by opening or unfolding a package of assorted color tissue papers. The excitement will grow as tissue overlays tissue on white paper or against the window light and as the children are encouraged to choose the overlapping colors and to identify the resulting hues.

To encourage color awareness and color exploration, the free-design, colored tissue collage is recommended for children of all ages. Using a sheet of white drawing or construction paper as a background surface, the youngsters cut or tear different colors, sizes, and shapes of tissue and paste them to the white background with either liquid laundry starch, polymer medium, or water-diluted Elmer's glue, overlapping the various shapes as they proceed. The teacher should suggest that they begin with the lighter colored tissues first and progress to darker values. It is difficult to change the dark colors by overlapping.

144

OPPOSITE PAGE. TOP—Tissue in assorted colors can be cut in smaller sizes and stored flat in shoe or shirt boxes. These youngsters are using rubber cement as the adhesive but liquid laundry starch is effective and more economical.

It is also recommended that the children first apply the paste or glue to the area they wish to cover with the tissue. Then the tissue piece should be placed down carefully over the moist areas and another coat of paste applied over it. Use a soft 1-inch or 1½-inch utility brush to apply the adhesive. Be sure that all loose edges are brushed down carefully.

As the children build and extend their compositions to the borders of the page, encourage them to look for unusual, hidden shapes of animals, birds, insects, fish, or fantastic figures. Once a form emerges and is identified, it can be heightened by adding torn pieces or strips of tissue in deeper colors to suggest or indicate arms, legs, horns, beaks, tails, hats, fins, and other appendages to give it significant character.

To emphasize the main form or figure, the background may be subdued by applying gray or white tissue over it. Crayon, felt-nib pen, colored watercolor marker, or tempera paint in white, gray, and black can be used to add exciting linear delineation to the figure or shape where desired, such as bark on a tree, scales on a fish, feathers on a bird, hair on an animal, or veins in a leaf. As an alternative, the positive shapes may remain unembellished while the background can be enriched with detail, pattern, and texture for contrast.

CENTER—Oil pastel linear composition and highlights were added after torn tissue was applied in bright patterns. Begin with light colored tissues. Grade 4, Iowa City, Iowa. BOTTOM—Black crayon or permanent black ink linear composition can be drawn first and torn or cut tissue applied freely over the lines. Sometime delineative lines can be re-inked after tissue dries.

This free-design approach with tissue is only one of many avenues open to children who wish to create in colored tissue. Another popular technique is the mixed-media collage. In this approach a preliminary drawing is made with crayon, waterproof felt-nib pen or magic marker on white drawing or construction paper or cream colored or white tagboard. After the drawing is completed, the cut or torn tissue is applied (as suggested earlier) to create the color effect. It is recommended that light-color tissues be applied first and that they be cut or torn slightly larger than the shape drawn. Sometimes when a number of layers of tissue are applied, the preliminary line drawing is obscured. However, when the tissue composition dries, some of these lines may be accented or emphasized by re-drawing them. Colored tissue used in conjunction with color sections and printed material of magazines is a very effective collage medium.

One last reminder. The storage of new and used tissue is a critical consideration. Tissue wrinkles or crumples very easily and this compounds storage problems. Encourage students to store it flat in designated boxes or drawers. Allow a liberal amount of time for clean-up and storage procedures.

Steps in a tissue collage. Visual inspiration is provided by a showing of color slides and beautifully illustrated books on insects. Color photography of natural forms by author Frank Wachowiak.

146

MOSAICS

The multifaceted technique of mosaic art, with its color segments called *tesserae,* has found its way into the elementary art program to enrich the design experiences of children. It is a welcome yet challenging addition to the repertoire of child expression. It sometimes involves special materials and tools, a longer time allotment, supplemental storage, and a teacher with sympathetic patience. Young children, however, can have success with the mosaic technique using such simple materials as colored construction paper, paste, and scissors. Upper-grade youngsters can carry the process further with vinyl, plastic, or ceramic tile obtained from scrap piles or discards.

Mounted birds and color-slide studies of owls by F. W. Kent, a nationally known photographer, provided rich stimulation for the sixth grade University School art class in Iowa City, Iowa. Flowers brought to school inspired other upper-grade youngsters to be individually creative in their mosaic projects (see next page).

149

Motivation for the project could include visits to contemporary mosaic mural installations in churches, civic centers, hospitals, hotels, banks, schools, or business offices. Color films that deal with mosaic art, past and present, from San Vitale, Rome to Watts Towers, Los Angeles should be shown when possible. Subject matter for mosaics that is simple yet exciting enough to interest young children might include: *Birds of Plumage, Birds in a Cage, Fish in the Sea, Animals in Their Habitats, A Flower Garden, Butterflies, Ships in Space.*

In mosaic design, as in all two-dimensional art expression, an important initial step is the preliminary sketch made from nature or life, from visits to natural museums, or from reference to films, slides, and photographs. These sketches are then developed into a satisfactory composition the size of the actual mosaic planned and transferred directly or with carbon paper to the chosen background material. Colored construction paper, railroad board in assorted colors, chipboard, oak tag, Masonite, or plywood can be utilized for this surface, depending on the mosaic process selected.

In the drawing, usually one object is emphasized but aspects of secondary emphases through repetition of the main motif, though on a smaller scale, could be included. The children should be encouraged to see and delineate characteristic features such as beaks on birds, horns on animals, fins and gills on fish. An effective contrast in the design to be translated in terms of the colored tesserae should be the goal.

One of the most critical factors in the success of a mosaic project is the effective organization of materials and tools. There must be an adequate supply of tesserae, whether it be paper, vinyl, or clay. In the case of colored construction paper, narrow strips of paper can be precut on the paper cutter and stored according to color in shoe boxes. The nature of vinyl, linoleum, or plastic material varies. Some can be cut with tinsnips. Others will have to be broken with a hammer. Upper-grade students should wear welder's goggles or swim masks as a precautionary measure when breaking hard vinyl. Sometimes the material can be put in a heavy canvas sack and broken. This is a much safer procedure.

Suggested adhesives for paper mosaic include partially diluted school paste, rubber cement, and white liquid glue. Adhesives for vinyl, glass, or ceramic mosaics include full strength white liquid glue and plastic or tile cement.

During a mosaic project, students should be instructed to take turns selecting the desired color strips or broken tesserae from the supply-table boxes. They may begin by pasting tesserae on a general area such as the sky or ground or they may concentrate first on a significant feature of the main figure—the beak of a bird, the horns of an animal, the pattern in a butterfly wing, or the petals of a flower. They should be guided to employ a varied application of the tesserae instead of a precise, brick-laying technique. The open spaces left between tesserae should vary somewhat for best effects.

Youngsters working together on a group project contributed individual segments to this colored construction paper mosaic panel of insects and flowers. Grades 3, 4, and 5, Athens, Georgia.

Tesserae should not be cut in exactly the same size. It will help if the paper strips originally cut on the paper cutter vary in width from ¼ to ¾ inch. They may be cut in irregular squares, rectangles, triangles, or multisided shapes. Rounded or curvilinear shapes are not recommended since they tend to negate the mosaic aesthetic, though their use may be warranted in other contexts.

The youngster may create excitement in his mosaic through a contrast of tessera colors in the various areas—the wing of a bird against the body, the stamen against the flower petal, an insect on a leaf. An important strategy in achieving mosaic quality is to employ several values of colored tesserae in the larger areas; for example, two or three blues in the sky, several greens in the grass, or many kinds of brown, umber, or ochre for earth tones. The brightest most intense colors can be reserved for rich emphasis as for instance in the beak or claw of a bird, the horns of a bull, the eyes of a cat, the stamen of a flower.

For vinyl, glass, or ceramic mosaics, where the tesserae are usually adhered to masonite or plywood, grouting is necessary. A workable homemade grout can be made with a dry mix of one-half powdered silica and one-half plaster of Paris (moulding plaster) or a mix of one-half marble dust and one-half plaster of Paris. A pure plaster of Paris may be used if supplements are unavailable. Dry tempera colors can be added to the plaster mix if desired. Sift the mix gradually into a partially filled container of water (a plastic dishpan works well) until islands of the plaster appear above the surface of the water. Then stir by hand and squeeze out lumps. When mixture begins to thicken to a creamy consistency, pour it on the center of the tesserated surface, then use the hands to spread or smooth the mixture evenly over the entire mosaic surface allowing it to settle between the tesserae. A sponge or rag may be used to remove the excess grout from the surface but the pressure should not be applied so heavily that the grout is dislocated from the interstices. A film of plaster will remain on the tesserae, but this can be removed when the grout is dry by scrubbing it off with a rag or soft brush. Grouted surfaces may be stained with oil, polymer, or acrylic colors if desired. Liquid or paste floor wax can be applied to completed vinyl mosaics to intensify the colors and protect the surface.

OPPOSITE PAGE—Colorful glass mosaic. Grade 6, Japan. A sheet of transparent contact paper sticky-side up is placed over the preliminary sketch in the bottom of a shallow container such as a paraffin-coated shoe or cigar box. Broken pieces of colored glass are then adhered to the paper in the mosaic design desired, allowing for spaces between each piece of glass. Plaster is mixed and poured over the completed glass design. When dry, pry the box apart, peel the contact paper off, and stain the plaster if desired. A hook may be put in the plaster before it dries.

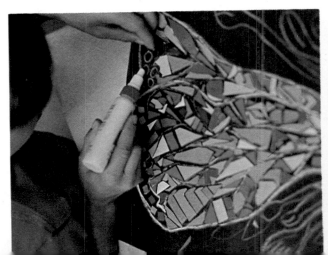

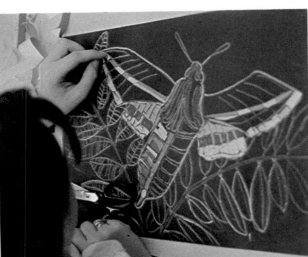

VEGETABLE PRINTS

Printmaking projects should be carefully programmed by the teacher so that they range from simple processes in the primary grades to complex techniques at the upper grades. Some of the most colorful, most exciting prints can be made by very young children using common, ordinary materials such as vegetables, fruit, leaves, bars of soap or paraffin, clay stamps, art gum erasers, as well as *found objects* such as buttons, flat wooden clothes pins, discarded wooden thread spools, bottle caps, mailing tubes, sponges, corks, and fingertips. Assorted vegetables and fruit (okra, peppers, mushrooms, oranges, artichokes, red cabbage, etc.) can be cut in half. The excitement grows when the students discover, perhaps for the first time, the beauty of the hidden design in these gifts from nature. The halved vegetables or fruit are then coated on the cut surface with tempera paint or pressed on a tempera moistened folded paper towel and then printed on a sheet of colored construction paper to form a repeat or free design.

154

CENTER—Potato and carrot print. Tempera paint on colored construction paper. BOTTOM—The same print with additional application of oil pastel. Note that some of the paper surface has been retained between the printed shapes and the pasteled areas. This, in effect, creates a kind of compositional unity. Grade 3 and 4, Athens, Georgia.

The most popular of the vegetable-print projects exploit the common potato as a printing stamp. The potato is cut in half with a paring knife and the flat surface is incised to create a relief. Children must be cautioned to exercise caution when using vegetable cutting tools. Recommended tools for use by primary youngsters are the black-handled Sloyd knife with its 2-inch blunt blade, the serrated plastic picnic knives which can be filed to a point at one end, metal fingernail files, and assorted nails. Melon ball scoops are excellent for creating circular effects. In the upper grades paring and scout knives, assorted linoleum gouges, and X-Acto knives may be introduced if employed with extreme care.

Youngsters should be encouraged to aim for a bold, simple break-up of space in their cut-out or incised designs. Suggest the exploitation of cross-cuts, wedges as in a pie, assorted sized holes, star, sunburst, and spiderweb effects, always keeping negative and positive design factors in mind.

The vegetables used must be fresh, crisp, and solid for controlled carving, cutting, and printing and should be refrigerated between sessions. A number of methods may be utilized to ink the cut vegetables, including direct brush application with tempera or watercolor; using a tempera-saturated printing pad made of several thicknesses of paper toweling; or rolling out water-base printing ink on a Masonite sheet, discarded serving tray, or cookie tin.

Construction paper in assorted colors is perhaps the most popular and most effective surface for vegetable printing, although other papers including colored tissue, newsprint, cream or gray manila, and wallpaper have been successfully used. A few practice prints on scrap sheets of colored construction paper are recommended. In some vegetable-print projects the child might be guided to develop a definite repeat pattern. In other instances the design can be left to the child's own inventiveness. Very often the imperfection or awkwardness of the youngster's efforts lends a naïve, spontaneous quality to the design. The children will discover that by sharing their vegetable stamps they can often produce exciting variations in their patterns and designs.

Vegetable prints have artistic merit in their simplest form, but they can often be embellished with other media to add richness and variety. One of the most successful of these augmentations is the application of varicolored oil pastel to the negative spaces between the printed shapes of the vegetables. Unity can be achieved by allowing some of the background colored construction paper to show between the pasteled areas and the printed shapes. Older students can carry the vegetable-print technique into even more complex undertakings by combining it with colored tissue overlays or as a tempera batik by applying India ink over the dry vegetable prints and next day rinsing the printed paper with water.

LEFT—Cutting relief design in potato. CENTER—Printing with tempera-painted vegetable. RIGHT—Youngsters learn to see hidden designs in vegetables cut in half. OPPOSITE PAGE—Vegetable prints on colored construction paper by youngsters. Grades 4 and 5, Athens, Georgia.

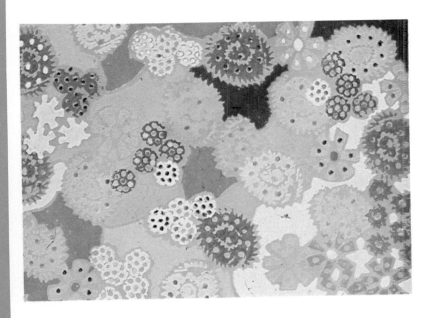 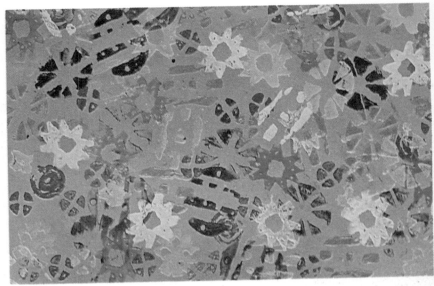

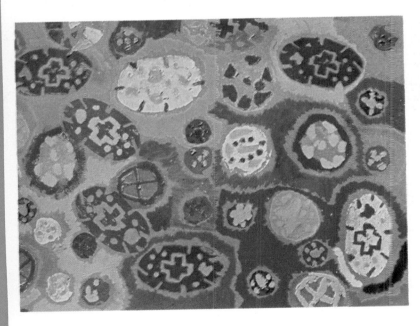 

157

GLUE LINE RELIEF PRINTS

A printmaking approach that is rather successful in all grades is the applied-glue line on cardboard print. It is a relatively simple technique but does require at least two working sessions because the glue must dry thoroughly before inking can be done. The youngsters will probably have to take their turns during the inking and printing stages, but a wise teacher will plan assignments for those who are waiting at their desks.

Materials required are smooth-surfaced cardboard (discarded glossy-surfaced box covers are excellent) or tagboard for the printing plate (plate sizes recommended are 9 by 9, 9 by 12, 12 by 12, or 12 by 18 inches); white liquid glue (Elmer's or Wilhold) in the plastic container with nozzle (if nozzle has not been pierced, it is preferable to use a pin to make the puncture so the glue does not flow out too generously); oil or water base ink (black is suggested); a soft rubber roller or brayer for inking; and an inking surface such as a 12 by 12 inch piece of tempered Masonite, a sheet of wax paper stretched and taped over a piece of plywood, or a discarded cookie tin; and newsprint or colored tissue paper.

OPPOSITE PAGE—White glue relief print. Size 12" x 18". Self portrait. Grade 1, Oshkosh, Wisconsin. THIS PAGE—Glue relief print. Size 12" x 18". Grade 6, Oshkosh.

159

Subject matter possibilities for glue prints are almost limitless. Young children will respond to birds, fish, flowers, insects, and animals as motifs. Students in the upper grades may choose more complex legendary, Biblical, historical, or space-science themes as well as still-life or cityscape compositions, portraits, or figure studies.

A preliminary drawing which is later transferred to the cardboard plate is definitely recommended. Suggest to the children that they keep the drawing bold and simple if possible. They should minimize the minute, intricate details that a pencil can make but which will blend together in the glue application and are often lost in the printing. On a 12 by 12 inch plate or cardboard it is wiser that the youngsters limit themselves to one large motif (bird, fish, animal, insect) and its complementary foliage rather than attempting several smaller shapes. In this way the child can delineate the characteristic features of eye, beak, claw, feather, or scale with the flowing glue.

When a satisfactory preliminary pencil sketch is completed, the child transfers it to the cardboard plate with carbon paper. Before the actual transfer, evaluate the composition with the youngster for a space-filling design, variety of shapes, exciting pattern, and avenues leading into the composition.

The cardboard plate is now ready for the application of the liquid glue. Holding the nozzle point of the glue container against the cardboard, the youngster gently squeezes the container trailing the glue over the drawn or traced line. With older children, the teacher may suggest that the thickness of the glue line be varied by controlling the pressure on the container, but in most instances a linear variety is achieved because it is difficult to manage a steady flow of glue.

The glue must be allowed to dry thoroughly before the cardboard plate can be inked. Some teachers suggest an overnight drying period. Designate an inking and printing area in the room. This could be a table or counter generously protected by newspapers. Demonstrate the application of the glue, the inking, printing, and wet-print storing procedures for the entire class. This will hopefully save a lot of time usually spent in individual instruction.

Squeeze out a ribbon of water-base printing ink on the inking slab. Roll out ink with brayer. Keep rolling until ink is tacky, then apply to the plate with a definite pressure. Roll on plate in both directions to be sure all parts of the plate are inked thoroughly. Then remove inked plate to the newspaper-covered printing area. Place a sheet of newsprint or colored tissue paper (slightly larger than the plate) over the plate carefully and apply pressure with the palm of the hand, beginning in the center of the plate and smoothing toward the edges.

If only a linear print is desired, the paper is placed over the inked plate and a rubber brayer is rolled carefully over the plate with an even pressure. Another possibility is to apply the frottage technique

TOP—Youngster draws preliminary sketch for his glue relief print. CENTER—Applying the glue over the drawn line on the tagboard plate. BOTTOM—A completed glue print.

161

in which a sheet of newsprint is placed over the clean, uninked plate and an inked brayer is rolled over the paper.

The most exciting glue prints are those in which the inked areas of the plate background as well as those of the glue lines are captured in the final print. To do this the youngster must use fingers, thumb, and heel of hand to press down on the paper between the raised glue lines as the print is taken. For the demonstration, the teacher should use white tissue because the children can see the actual absorption of the ink into the paper and can detect areas that need more pressure to be effective. Sometimes the initial print is not completely satisfactory because the plate itself absorbs so much ink. The second print is usually more successful.

Wet prints can be stored on the floor or counters around the room or hung on clothesline cord with spring clothespins.

The plate itself can be embellished further, matted, and displayed. It can be given a coat of ink or paint and partially rinsed off for an unusual wet effect. It can be coated with polymer medium then stained with Rub'n'Buff commercial patinas in green, copper, silver, or gold; a sheet of aluminum foil can be placed over the plate overlapping the edges and pressed firmly with fingers to bring out the relief lines, much like a metal repoussé. Apply a coat of India ink or black enamel to the foil and when dry burnish with steel wool to bring out the highlights.

Nature's forms lend themselves beautifully to glue-print designs. Grade 5, Oshkosh, Wisconsin. Some teachers have discovered that 4-inch-wide house paint rollers can be employed to apply black tempera or water-base ink to the glue relief plates.

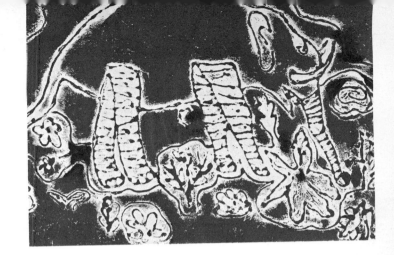

A simpler method of giving the aluminum-covered plate dark and light values is to roll an ink-covered rubber brayer over the metal relief. This provides a similar effect to a standard print but with the added sparkle of the aluminum highlights. Aluminum-covered glue relief plates can be attractively matted or framed.

One final suggestion. Youngsters who are waiting their turn to ink and print their plates might find it interesting to make a crayon or oil pastel rubbing of their plate. This can be accomplished by putting a sheet of newsprint or tissue over the plate, holding it firmly, and rubbing across it carefully but firmly with the side of a black or dark-colored crayon or oil pastel. This is not suggested as a substitute for the inked print, but opens up another avenue of expression.

TOP LEFT—Preliminary sketch for a glue print. Grade 5, Lawton Elementary School, Ann Arbor, Michigan. RIGHT CENTER—Youngsters utilized a class model for this complex print. Grade 6, Athens, Georgia. RIGHT TOP and BOTTOM—Grades 2 and 3, Lakewood and Martin Luther Elementary Schools, Ann Arbor, Michigan.

COLLOGRAPHS

When youngsters reach the upper elementary level, they become interested in and challenged by more complex, more technically demanding approaches to printmaking. Cardboard prints, sometimes referred to as collographs, which can be created with commonly available materials and simple, nonhazardous tools offer this kind of variety, excitement, and exploitation. The final results are often similar to wood or linoleum block prints. The flexibility of rearranging or changing the composition of the print before the final gluing of the separate cardboard shapes is a significantly welcome feature of this print technique.

For children with little previous experience in the technique, the following materials and tools are suggested: a piece of cardboard (the lid or bottom section of a shirt or stationery box, chipboard, scrap Masonite discards, heavy tagboard), glue, scissors, paper punch, ink brayer or roller, water-base printing ink, newsprint paper or colored tissue, shellac, 1-inch utility brush, and solvent for shellac.

OPPOSITE PAGE—The collograph lends itself well to story-telling illustrations. This is a Japanese child's version of "The Pied Piper of Hamelin." THIS PAGE. TOP— Note how negative as well as positive shapes were used. Grade 5, Oshkosh, Wisconsin.

165

Subject matter themes for cardboard prints are limitless. They can be anything the child sees, remembers, or imagines. However, there should be the same concern for a strong composition that is given to any other graphic design project. Especially important is the emphasis on effective utilization of a variety of cut-out shapes to fill the space of the cardboard surface the child has chosen. A recommended plate size for this intermediate age group is a sheet 9 by 9, 9 by 12, or 12 by 12 inches or circles and ovals in approximately the same dimensions. Pieces much larger than this create a management problem in crowded classes, especially during the inking, printing, and drying phases. Storage of work in progress is a critical factor. The use of large envelopes or folders labeled with the child's name is recommended during the early cutting and gluing stage.

When the youngsters have drawn and cut out the separate, individual shapes from the oak tag, tagboard, manila, corrugated paper, butcher's tape, masking tape, and assorted weight papers and have created open patterns in some of these shapes employing the paper punch, X-Acto knives, single-edge razor blades, and pinking shears, they arrange these elements on the background sheet until a satisfactory composition is obtained. Some pieces may overlap each other for unity and interest, however, the relief should not be built up too high. When the youngster, with the teacher's guidance, achieves a satisfying, space-filling design, he carefully glues the separate pieces to the plate surface. It is very important

Steps in making a collograph. TOP—Cutting or tearing the separate parts. CENTER—Gluing down the parts securely. After gluing, apply a sealing protective coat of shellac or white glue. BOTTOM—Inking the plate.

that all edges of applied pieces be glued down very securely. The whole composition is then given a coat of shellac or polymer medium to seal it thus preventing the separately-glued pieces from dissolving and coming loose during the printing or cleaning phase. A separate table or counter covered with newspapers should be designated as a shellac-application area. Store shellacked compositions out of the students' way, preferably in a well-ventilated area, and allow to dry thoroughly.

The inking and printing phase of this project is naturally the most exciting stage for the youngsters, but unless the teacher has planned this segment of the activity carefully, it can develop into chaotic bedlam.

Final step in the collograph, pulling the print. If water-base printing ink is used, don't wait too long to pull the print because the ink dries quickly and the paper will stick to it.

The teacher should have on hand several inking surfaces (1 foot square pieces of tempered Masonite, discarded cookie tins or cafeteria trays, scrap squares of formica), soft rubber brayers or ink rollers, 3 or more inches wide, water-base printing inks, newsprint paper, brown wrapping paper, assorted colored thin poster or colored tissue papers.

In a typical classroom situation, it is suggested that an inking and printing table covered with newspapers be set up where three to four students can work at a time. Let them attempt a single-color print first, perhaps black. Later the students might try a multicolor print. Roll the ink carefully on the plate in both directions using even pressure. Take the inked plate to a clean surface. Place a sheet of newsprint over the inked plate and rub with the palm of the hand. Press down at the corners and edges. Use fingers or heel of hand to press areas between the pasted shapes. Where you want print to be dark, press hardest. Do not wait too long to remove print from plate. Water-base inks dry quickly and paper may stick to plate. Lift newsprint off carefully and store to dry. All wet prints should be put on shelves, spring-clipped to a clothesline, or lined along the counters or baseboard where youngsters will not disturb them.

TOP—Collograph. Grade 3, Iowa City, Iowa. BOTTOM—Grade 2, Japan.

The process of inking and pulling a print should be demonstrated step-by-step for the whole class so that it does not have to be repeated for each student in turn. Care must be taken when washing the plate. Sometimes it is wiser to let the ink remain on it to dry overnight. Additional prints may be made from a plate that has been inked and dried.

Finished prints can be attractively mounted for display purposes. Children may exchange prints. The plate itself can be inked in two or three colors, mounted, framed, and displayed.

Children in the fifth and sixth grades can exploit the cardboard print technique even further through the use of a variety of materials to create linear and textural print quality. Suggested effects include decorative tape, string, gummed reinforcements, textured wall paper, liquid glue, plus a variety of *found objects*.

Third-grade youngsters combined their efforts to make this collograph mural. Theme: "Animals in the Jungle."

LINOLEUM PRINTS

A technically challenging form of graphic expression recommended for the upper elementary grades is linoleum block printing, sometimes referred to as lino printing. Unmounted, pliable linoleum suggested for this project may be obtained from art supply firms. In some instances it is available from furniture or department stores but the teacher should make certain it is the pliable kind that can be easily cut and not the brittle, hard-surfaced plastic type. The basic materials and tools needed include a set of lino cutting gouges, a rubber brayer (ink roller), an inking surface (a piece of Masonite, a cookie tin, a serving tray, or wax paper stretched over a sheet of plywood), printing ink (oil or water-base), and assorted papers such as colored construction, tissue, newsprint, brown wrapping, newspaper, wallpaper, and colored pages from magazines. A special inking and printing area covered with newspapers should be provided in the classroom.

OPPOSITE PAGE—Linoleum print inspired by museum sketches. Grade 5, Iowa City, Iowa. THIS PAGE—Wood block prints by Japanese children. Grades 4 and 5. Note how much was observed and recorded in these beautiful black and white compositions.

171

Youngsters in the third grade are shown gouging a lino block and preparing the colored tissue background for a linoleum print. The tissue may also be applied with liquid laundry starch to a sheet of white construction paper. Some of the children printed their lino plates on magazine ads. Heavy pressure must be used to achieve a good print when employing tissue collage background.

Preliminary drawings and sketches in pencil, black crayon, pen and ink, brush and ink, white crayon on black paper, or felt-nib ink marker are important requisites for a successful printmaking project because they often determine the final composition, including the dark and light pattern, the variety of textural exploitation, the areas of emphasis, and the lines of motion.

The teacher and the students must be cognizant of the fact that each particular lino gouge makes its own unique incisions and indentures and although it does not lend itself to the same control as the pencil or pen, it often produces linear effects that are more direct, honest, and dynamic. The various gouges, from veiners to scoops to shovels, should be exploited to the fullest extent to achieve both linear and mass effects.

The color print above is the result of an interesting experiment. The student prints his lino plate employing oil-base black ink on a piece of clear acetate (bleached X-ray plates are suggested) and then places the acetate print over vari-colored paper. Different magazine ad backgrounds may be exploited. Grade 4, Oshkosh, Wisconsin.

173

Subject matter themes for lino prints are unlimited, but students will discover rich sources for exciting compositions and textural exploitation in rare birds, jungle animals, insects, fish, old houses, cityscapes, legendary or mythological figures, portraits, and still-life arrangements composed of sports equipment, musical instruments, plants, lanterns, antiques, household utensils, and similar items.

After a preliminary sketch has been made, the youngster may use it as a reference to draw directly on the lino plate or he may transfer his sketch to the lino surface with carbon paper. He should be reminded that the final print is always the reverse of the sketch. He may, if he wishes, reverse the sketch before transferring it to the plate. If the lino surface is a dark color, it may be painted with white latex or polymer paint before the sketch is transferred. Sometimes the preliminary pencil sketch can be transferred to the block by putting the sketch, pencil-side down, on the block and rubbing over it with a metal spoon. In this case the final print is compositionally the same as the sketch.

There are various methods recommended for cutting the lino block. The veiners or v-shaped gouges #1 and #2 are suggested to make the initial outline of the composition. Another approach is to use the scoop or shovel gouges working from the inside of the shapes, thus minimizing the tightly outlined composition.

Sometimes the student can avoid mistakes in cutting by marking an "X" in those areas of the block that are to be gouged out. It is recommended that the youngster employ directional gouge cuts by following the contour of the object he is delineating. Backgrounds, too, can be gouged out in directional strokes around an object much like ripples around a pebble tossed in a stream. The students should be cautioned not to cut too deeply into the linoleum. The low ridges remaining can produce a unique textural effect.

In large classes and in situations where materials are limited, proofs of the blocks in process can be obtained in an economical, effective manner by placing a sheet of newsprint or onionskin paper over the cut-out block, and with the side of a black crayon or oil pastel rub over the paper with a steady and even pressure. The result is a definitive proof which can furnish the youngster with clues to his progress.

Either water- or oil-base printing inks may be used for the final prints. Oil ink is generally recommended for best results, but water-base ink is suggested for situations where expeditious clean-up is a vital factor. The ink may be rolled out with a rubber brayer on a discarded cookie tin or serving tray, on wax paper taped to a sheet of plywood, on a piece of tempered Masonite, or on a commercially available inking slab. When the ink feels tacky, it is applied to the linoleum block.

There are a number of ways to take or "pull" a print. The youngster may place the paper carefully on the inked block which has been removed to a clean area. He applies strong and even pressure with a brayer, the heel of a metal tablespoon, a commercial baren, or the heel of the hand. Pull off the paper carefully from the block. If water-base ink is used, the process must be speeded up because the ink dries swiftly and the paper may stick. A commercial block-printing press is a welcome asset in printmaking where the budget provides for one.

A variety of background papers may be used for lino prints. These include newsprint, brown or white wrapping paper (available in 36-inch wide rolls), colored construction or tissue paper, gray or cream manila paper, and colored pages or advertisements from magazines. A most effective way to display or exhibit lino block prints is to mat them allowing a slight margin to show between the mat and the border of the print. They can also be mounted against bright colored construction paper but be sure to allow for generous borders.

CLAY

Every child in the elementary school should have the opportunity to create and express his ideas in clay. Clay is malleable, flexible, and pliable, yet at the same time it is unpredictable, resisting, and often messy. Some youngsters respond to clay more enthusiastically than others but all children can benefit from the unique challenge of this earthy material.

The very young child in the primary grades is a natural clay manipulator. He needs very little encouragement as he pokes, squeezes, pounds, stretches, rolls, and pinches the moist clay. He enjoys exploring all its possibilities.

No two youngsters will tackle clay modeling in the same manner. Some may pull out shapes from a ball or lump of clay; some may add pieces to the basic form. Some may begin a figure with the main body structure; others may start with appendages and head.

The teacher's main responsibility at this early stage is to provide the child with an adequate supply of workable clay. A ball of clay the size of a grapefruit is recommended for each child. Offer some suggestions for the protection of desk or table tops and introduce just enough stimulating motivation to get the youngster started.

176

A short period of exploration and experimentation with the clay should precede every clay project. This is especially true in the upper grades. Youngsters need to get the feel of the clay before they can express a particular idea. During this orientation session, the teacher might call their attention to the desired plasticity of the clay, the necessity of keeping excess clay moist by rolling the crumbs into a single ball, and the mechanics of clay clean-up.

One way to introduce young children to the feel and the potential of clay is to initiate the "clay in a paper sack game." Give each child a ball of clay about the size of a grapefruit or orange and a paper sack. Tell them to put the clay in the sack and without looking inside, manipulate the clay in the bag until they feel they have made an interesting shape. Ask them to think with their hands. Encourage them to stretch the clay, to pull on it, to pinch it, to squeeze it, to poke it with the fingers. Above all they must not peek inside the bag until they have completed the manipulation. The finished pieces may be displayed on the desks or counters for all the students to see. Ask the youngsters: In what way are the clay forms the same? How are they different? Does anyone see the form of an animal, bird, or fish in the clay? What did we learn about clay?

These fantastic clay constructions, like some undersea castles, are the imaginative expressions of Japanese school children. Grades 2 and 3. Clay is employed very widely in the Japanese elementary school program.

The animal kingdom provides a wealth of inspiration for the young artist. Four-legged mammals such as cows, horses, elephants, hippos, and bears are especially recommended because the child can make them stand up with ease. Other popular animals to model in clay are rabbits, turtles, squirrels, and alligators. Group projects with themes such as *Noah's Ark*, *Three-Ring Circus*, *The Zoo*, *The Farm*, and *The Jungle* are very popular with young children. Human figures are a little more difficult for them to master, unless the child is guided to provide additional supports or construct thick, sturdy legs that will hold the figure in balance.

The primary child is especially interested in the mobility and adaptability of the clay. He may tell a whole story with one figure, such as a clown, manipulating it to create various postures. His clown might stand on his head, bend backwards, or fall down. Clay for the young child fulfills a definite kinesthetic and story-telling need.

The animal world is the joy and delight of the child who models in clay.

178

Some technical assistance may have to be given the young child who experiences difficulty with his clay construction. For the child who has a tendency to pat his clay into a flat cookie shape, suggest that he cup the ball of clay in his hands as he forms the body and head of the animal, bird, or fish he is making. In this way he will have more success in achieving a three-dimensional mass. Once he has modeled the characteristic shape of the animal, he can pull out or add arms, legs, tails, trunks, horns, and tusks.

The teacher might suggest a simple way to make the appendages adhere strongly to the main body by inserting them into holes made in the clay with the fingers. For youngsters who are in the upper grades the process of scoring and welding can be demonstrated and explained. Supplementary clay supports to counteract sagging form, such as a fifth leg under the animal's body, can be suggested. When the clay is leather-hard, this support can be removed. At all times the teacher should emphasize the importance of working for a simple, sturdy, yet characteristic interpretation.

TOP—The youngster who holds the clay ball in his hand can make a truly three-dimensional bird. RIGHT—Note how massive these clowns' legs are to hold up their bodies. Children learn they must make strong legs, or add a third support, to make their figures stand strong.

179

Though many children in the primary grades are not concerned with details as such, there will always be a number who find excitement in experimenting with textures and patterned relief on their clay creations. A collection of *found objects* such as popsicle sticks, bottle caps, nails, screws, plastic forks and spoons, buttons, shells, bark, beads, round wood clothespins, wrapping cord, combs, toothbrushes, and pieces of wire mesh will spark interest in decorative possibilities. All *found objects* should be washed or cleaned thoroughly before each usage.

When youngsters reach the third and fourth grades, they are often more successful in mastering the challenging complexities of advanced clay modeling. However, they may ask for specific help with the problems of figures and appendages that sag or come apart, with balance and proportion, with intricate delineation, and with features such as eyes, mouths, ears, beaks, snouts, and horns.

Found objects can be exploited for making patterns and texture in clay.

At this stage a number of effective motivations may be included in the teaching repertoire: field trips to observe and sketch animals at a farm, ranch, zoo, animal shelter, or natural museum; family pets brought to class as models; photographs of animals; films on animals in their habitats; and large reproductions of drawings, paintings, and sculptures of animals by artists of many countries. If the project involves the making of pottery, a visit to a college ceramic department or to a contemporary potter's studio will whet student interest and provide authoritative answers to pertinent questions.

As a subject for clay sculpture, the prehistoric dinosaur fires the imagination of children, especially of those youngsters who are developing a strong interest in natural science and in the wonders of the universe. The theme of the earth's primeval giants intrigues the child. Perhaps he has read that the bones of some prehistoric monster have been found in his own region. He may even have seen the colossal, reconstructed skeletons in a museum of natural history. The dinosaur, indeed, is uniquely adapted to interpretation in clay—the characteristic mass of the creature, ponderous, monumental, armorlike, its rough, eroded, wrinkled skin evoking the quality of the elemental earth itself.

A preliminary drawing for clay projects in the upper grades is optional. Quite often, however, it helps the youngster clarify his visual concept of the animal or figure he plans to model. For a clay dinosaur project the teacher may have to allot a greater amount of clay to each student than suggested for primary grade clay activities. In any case, extra prepared clay should always be ready for emergencies.

For those students who need help in undertaking their clay dinosaur, a fundamental body structure based on the post and lintel technique is suggested. A lump of clay slightly larger than a grapefruit is rolled out into a thick, heavy coil to form body, tail, neck, and sometimes the head of the dinosaur. For the legs, four or more rolled coils of clay are attached securely to the body. Make holes in the body structure with a finger and push the appendages into them, then strengthen the junctures with additional clay. No armature supports such as wire, sticks, twigs or reed should be used inside the structure in order to prevent uneven shrinkage or cracking. This is especially to be avoided if the clay will be fired.

Planned preliminary discussions by students and teacher should center on the structural possibilities that can give character to the dinosaur—the sway of the body, the stance and counterstance of the legs, the swing of the tail, the turn of the head, the flow of the mane, the action of jaws, and the flare of wings. In some instances a highly imaginatively expressive dinosaur may combine the characteristics of a number of different prehistoric monsters. At all stages during the modeling, the clay animal should be viewed from every side so that the youngster can develop the form as three-dimensionally as possible. A 1-foot square Masonite working base will help make this possible.

There are almost no limits to clay relief and textural exploitation where older children are involved. Whether their creation is a clay pot, a bas-relief, a figure, an animal, or a nonobjective design, the field of decoration is wide open. The *found object* collection will provide a welcome source of texture-making tools. To achieve the scaly and armorlike skin of certain dinosaurs, students might roll out balls, coils, and ribbons of clay and apply them to the main body of the animal. Slip (water-diluted clay) can be used as an adhesive to secure the pellets or strips of clay. Discarded broken saw blades, pencils, beads, plastic forks, cord, and assorted hardware can be used to incise and impress unique textural effects. Discourage the use of scissors, compasses, and similar tools which can be ruined by rust.

Man and animal have always intrigued the child as a motif for clay projects. Teachers should build on this natural interest.

If a kiln is available and the animals are to be fired, they should be allowed to dry evenly and slowly until leather-hard. They may be stored to dry in a cabinet or on a counter under a sheet of plastic which can be gradually removed. In the case of large animals, holes or hollows should be made in their understructures while the piece is still leather-hard. These apertures allow the moisture to escape and prevent cracking or exploding of the clay during the firing.

Kiln glazing of the fired clay pieces is rarely undertaken in the elementary school because of limited budgets and firing facilities. However, there are other avenues to the enrichments of bisque or fired clay. Among these, staining is definitely recommended for projects in the upper grades. Shoe polish, wood stains, powder paint, enamel colors, oil pastels, white glue, moist dirt, Rub'n'Buff, and latex paint are among the possibilities for applying a finish or patina to the bisque ware. Liquid floor wax is suggested as a protective coat. Sometimes it is wise to limit the colors used or to neutralize the colors. In all cases remind the students that the colors applied should add to, rather than detract from, their work.

At the fifth- and sixth-grade levels, more sophisticated clay projects can be programmed. Pots combining pinch, coil, patch, and slab procedures can now challenge the more serious students. Bas-reliefs, mosaic, bells, bird feeders, hanging ash trays, light fixtures, and complex figure-and-animal combinations will keep the growing youngster interested in ceramic art at this critical stage in his development.

TOP—This 14-inch high pot was built using the double pinch pot technique. Pinch pots were joined together into hollow spheres and then the two spheres were paddled into more organic shapes and joined together. A foot and neck were added. BOTTOM—Detail shows how texture was achieved by employing clay slabs, pellets, and impressions made into the clay with found objects. Grade 5.

183

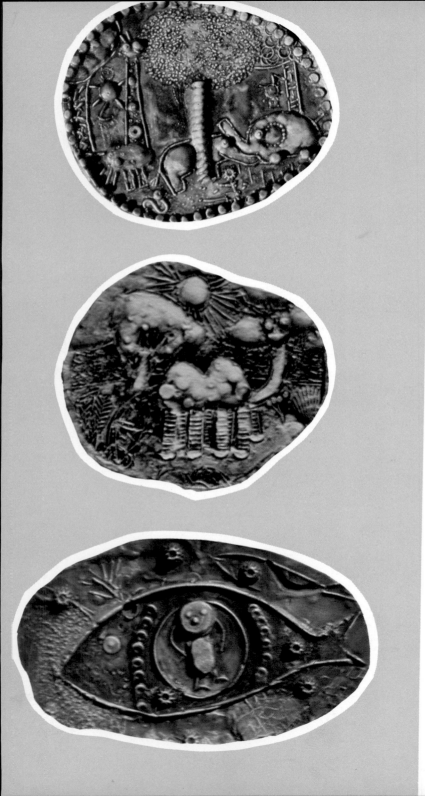

PLASTER RELIEF

Youngsters in the upper grades are often self-critical of their drawing ability and need the satisfaction and challenge of creating in art media not always dependent on drawing or painting skills. Techniques involving manipulative materials and special tools whet their expressive appetites, and even though a simple, preliminary sketch is recommended for a particular object, the fact that it can be freely interpreted and changed in the ensuing process often insures their enthusiastic approval.

Art projects that belong in this category are lino prints, wood block prints, metal repoussé, ceramics, subtractive sculpture, papier-mâché, stitchery, metal enameling, and constructions involving *found objects*. A popular project that youngsters respond to, and have success with, is the plaster relief.

For a relief sculpture in this medium the following materials and tools are recommended: moist earth clay; plaster; a plastic dishpan; a container for the clay mold (shoe box, cigar box, half-gallon or gallon milk carton), an assortment of discarded or *found objects* of all kinds—spools, nails, wire lath, screws, keys, bottle caps, buckles, round wooden clothespins, rope, cord, beads, reed, plastic forks and spoons, as well as natural objects such as twigs, pine cones, acorns, nuts, sea shells and bark; a plaster sealing medium (Elmer's or Wilhold glue, shellac), 1-inch wide utility brush; and staining liquids (wood stains, diluted oil paints, shoe stains).

The Jungle and the Bible provided subject themes for these plaster plaques. BOTTOM—"Jonah in the Whale." Grade 4, Iowa City, Iowa.

The first step in the project is to prepare the box for the clay mold. In the case of a shoebox, simply reinforce the box with a strip of masking tape around the top edge. Put the lid under the box to reinforce that area. The inside of the box may be coated with melted paraffin or lined with wax paper. If a milk carton is used, cut in half lengthwise. If the open end is resealed with tape, both halves of the carton may be used. No protective coat is needed. In the case of the cigar box, remove lid and coat inside with paraffin.

Two methods of making the basic clay mold are suggested. In the simplest procedure, the clay is rolled out in a slab approximately $\frac{1}{2}$ to 1 inch thick, cut to the size of the box, and placed in the bottom of the box ready for the next stage. In the second method, the clay is placed in the bottom of the box, piece by piece, until the bottom is filled to a depth of $\frac{1}{2}$ to 1 inch. If a very flat clay surface is desired, the clay may be stamped with a piece of lumber.

Before the students begin their impressions in the clay mold, they should practice designs on a small slab of clay using various imprinting tools. Discussion and demonstration should reveal that an impression made in the clay will be the reverse in the plaster cast. Designs pressed in will bulge out. Letters, numbers, and names must be imprinted backwards in order to read correctly in the final product.

In some instances, by putting a clay wall around a student's practice clay piece and filling it with plaster, the teacher can take a quick cast to show the class what happens in the casting. Knowing the limits and the possibilities of this exciting medium frees the student to be more innovative, more expressive.

There are a number of ways to build the clay negative mold. A very free and natural approach may involve the use of hands and fingers. Commercial ceramic tools may also be employed. Coils, pellets, and ribbons of clay out cut from a thin slab may be applied with slip.

With younger children it might be wise to limit the design or subject matter to those ideas that can be best expressed with the impressions of the *found objects* available. In this approach, instead of scratching or incising lines in the clay with a nail or stick, a procedure which produces sharp and troublesome edges in the final plaster cast, the child *presses* his lines into the clay. For straight lines he may use reed, applicator sticks, edge of popsickle stick, or the edge of a piece of cardboard. For curved lines he might use bent reed, cord, string, bent wire. Children of all ages enjoy the variety of textures and pattern they can create through the combination of the various imprinting objects.

Subject matter themes for plaster reliefs include imaginative birds, fish, insects, animals in their habitats, flower gardens, legendary or Biblical figures, heraldic devices, personal insignia, and nonobject designs.

When the composition or design is completed in the clay, the liquid plaster mix is poured over it to approximately ½ to 1 inch in thickness. Before the plaster sets, a bent paper clip or circle of wire may be inserted into it to provide a hanging hook for the completed plaster relief. For a concise explanation on plaster-mixing procedures, see the following section on subtractive sculpture. Allow sufficient time for the plaster to set. This may vary from ½ to 1 or more hours. Some teachers suggest letting the plaster dry overnight.

When the plaster is hard, the student pries open the cardboard container or carton and separates the clay from the plaster. If this separation is made carefully, most of the moist clay in the mold can be saved for another project.

To prepare the plaster relief for the staining or glazing, the youngster should file, cut, or sand excess edges and sharp points that might be abrasive. The relief can then be washed with water. A discarded toothbrush can be used to clean the clay out of recessed areas. Before staining, give the plaster relief a generous coat of slightly water-diluted white glue, nondiluted polymer medium, or clear shellac. Let this coating dry thoroughly.

The most successful color stains for this project are wood stains, shoe stains, or oil paints generously diluted with turpentine. Oil colors recommended are raw umber, burnt umber, raw sienna, burnt sienna, ochre, and earth green. If bright colors are employed, they should be dulled by their complements. Apply the stains with a small utility brush, let the paint flow into the indentations and incisions, then wipe off the surface with a soft cloth to bring out highlights.

For situations where color staining of the reliefs is impractical, the dry plaster may be tinted by mixing it with powder paints before sifting it into the water and pouring the cast.

Plaster reliefs are a definite *must* for elementary teachers and their students who are looking for exciting, challenging art projects.

The clay negative mold and completed plaster positive relief are illustrated above. Note that a reverse image results and that shapes impressed into the clay bulge out in the plaster relief. A sea shell was pressed into the clay for the elephant's ears. A string of beads, round wooden clothespin, and bottle cap were other indenting objects employed. Grade 3, Iowa City, Iowa.

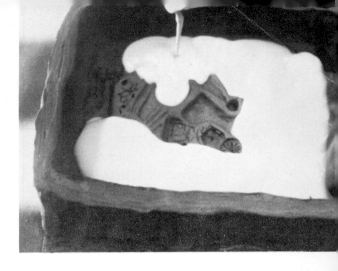

Steps in creating a plaster relief. TOP LEFT—Making the clay mold by impressing objects into the clay slab. TOP RIGHT—Pouring the plaster into the clay mold. Plaster should be of a creamy consistency. BOTTOM LEFT—Separating dried plaster relief from clay mold. Wash plaster relief and coat with white glue. BOTTOM RIGHT—Stain dried plaster relief with shoe or wood stains. Apply stain with brush. Rub off highlights with cloth.

SCULPTURE

Subtractive sculpture in semihard materials can prove an exciting and rewarding art technique for upper-grade children if it is introduced as a serious and aesthetic challenge. Too often it has been presented in a superficial manner with minor emphasis on its three-dimensional potential.

If sufficient time cannot be allotted in the school schedule for the youngsters to become thoroughly involved in the sculptural process (this will vary from 2 to 4 hours and may have to be extended in some cases), then it should be postponed until the junior high or middle-school years. However, if the teacher understands some of the possibilities and the limitations of the sculptural medium and the students are sufficiently motivated to tackle the technique and carry it to its rewarding culmination, the experience can be one of the most fulfilling in the program.

Recommended and quite readily obtainable materials for subtractive sculpture projects are molding plaster, foamglass, soap, sand core, porous, lightweight firebrick, and wax. Commercially available products specifically recommended for carving include Featherrock, Crea-stone, and Carvit stone.

Subject ideas for sculpture that youngsters can handle quite successfully include fish, birds, animals (especially those in repose) portraits or imaginary heads, organic and nonobjective form including motifs based on rocks, shells, nuts, and other natural or biomorphic inspiration.

188

Three different animals carved from a prepared plaster block to which fine zonolite had been added. TOP—Seal with white glue and coat with a walnut wood stain. BOTTOM— Seal with white glue; then, using bristle brush, coat with Sculpmetal. When dry, paint with India ink. Finally, burnish with steel wool. Grade 6, Iowa City, Iowa.

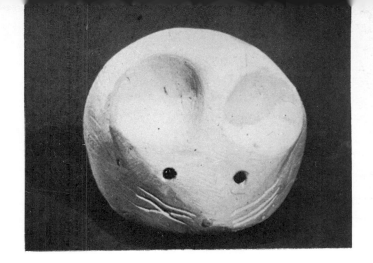

If plaster is selected as the medium, it should be mixed with additives such as fine grain zonolite or sand to give it texture and make it easier to carve. One part of additive to one part of plaster will produce a fairly porous and workable block. A half-gallon or quart size waxed-paper milk carton makes an adequate container for molding the block.

While the students are making preliminary sketches (optional) of their sculpture, the teacher can supervise two or more students at a time in the making of the plaster molds. At a newspaper-covered table or counter near the sink if possible, all the necessary materials should be available: plaster, zonolite or sand, metal or plastic scoops, wax milk cartons opened wide at top, water, rubber or pliable plastic dishpan, wood stick, dry tempera colors if desired. Newspapers should cover the floor around the mixing area and line the wastebaskets near at hand.

Fill milk carton three-quarters full with water. Pour this water into dishpan. Sift plaster into water slowly using hand or a scoop. When islands of plaster appear above the water, add zonolite or sand. Stir gently yet swiftly with hand, squeezing the lumps until thoroughly mixed. Mixture thickens very quickly, so pour immediately into milk carton. Tap plaster-filled carton on the table to remove trapped air bubbles or stir quickly with a long stick or wooden spatula. Excess plaster left in dishpan should be scraped into newspaper-lined wastebasket. *Do not pour down the sink!* Let the plaster mold harden completely. This may take 1 to 2 hours or more. In most cases teachers allow it to dry overnight. If color is desired in the plaster mold, dry tempera colors may be used to tint the dry plaster before it is mixed with water. Colors such as umber, ochre, sienna, earth green, and turquoise blue are recommended.

Some teachers have discovered that a sturdy plastic bag can be used as a container for the plaster carving block. Sculpture above from Milwaukee Public Schools. A noted wood carver was once asked how he created his renowned horses. His answer: "I carve away everything that doesn't look like a horse."

The student may transfer his sketches to the block with carbon paper or draw directly on the block with pencil. He may prefer to carve directly using his sketch as a reference only. If he uses a sketch, he cuts, files, rasps, or chisels away the excess plaster to delineate the profile view. Next he may use his top, front, and rear sketches and cut into his block to define those contours. He should proceed slowly and cautiously as he removes the excess plaster. The best tools for this process are the Sloyd or Hyde knife with the 2-inch semisharp blade, the open plaster rasp, or the hammer and chisel. At this stage the youngster should keep turning his sculpture piece around to define masses consistently. Working areas should be covered with newspapers to expedite clean-up.

The teacher should help the student evaluate his work in process: to be aware of large shapes contrasting against small shapes; to see that one form flows gracefully into another; to capture the characteristic gesture or action; to emphasize a significant feature such as the beak or claws of a bird, the gill of a fish, or the horns of a bull; to enrich the surface through textures and pattern used sensitively and economically.

Nails, discarded dental tools, and nut picks are very effective for incising lines and descriptive detail. When the carving and delineation are complete, the sculpture may be stained, glazed, antiqued, or waxed if desired. To provide a working surface for the stain or patina, the plaster piece should be coated or sealed with an application of white liquid glue or polymer medium. Allow this coating to dry thoroughly.

Perhaps the simplest method of staining the piece is to apply one of the many wood stains available. These come in a variety of subtle colors including a new dark earth green. Apply the stain freely with utility brush and let it penetrate into the incised or textured areas of the plaster. Allow to set briefly and then wipe off raised areas with a cloth to bring out highlights. If stain did not penetrate incised designs, re-incise those areas and stain again. Tube oil paints diluted with turpentine to a liquid consistency may also be used as staining agents.

Sometimes the most honest, direct approach in carving is best. Primitive peoples sculpted objects to use in their everyday lives. Form followed function beautifully. The African horse and rider carved in wood, above, is an example of the honesty, integrity, restraint, and understatement that timeless sculpture evokes. Collection of Mr. and Mrs. Chet LaMore, Ann Arbor, Michigan.

PAPIER-MÂCHÉ TECHNIQUES

Most children in the upper grades possess the technical and manipulative skills that papier-mâché processes demand. However, the teacher should have all necessary materials organized beforehand—newspapers, string, wire, tape, wheat paste, liquid laundry starch, paint, colored tissue, yarn—whatever she plans to incorporate into the project. She must also arrange for storage of papier-mâché figures in process. Techniques a teacher might choose for her students, depending on class size, time allotted, materials available, and theme selected, include: A framework of rolled newspapers secured with string or masking tape (see below). Covering blown-up balloons or light bulbs attached to plastic bottles. Stuffing paper sacks with newspaper and tying with string to create head and body. Using wire or wooden armatures (a basic skeletal form). Modeling with chicken or screen wire when group projects lead to large forms. In the illustrations, right, by classroom teachers the students drilled holes in a wood base and secured their wire and newspaper roll armature into these holes which made the construction much easier to control. Note the colorfully coordinated painted design on both the animal and the base. Courtesy Oliver Coleman, University of Georgia, Athens, Georgia.

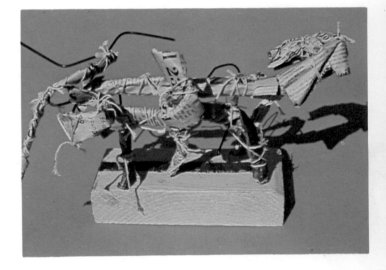

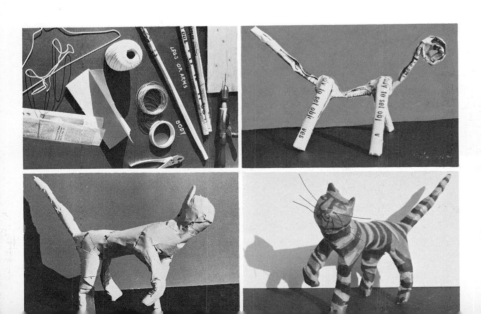

CONSTRUCTIONS IN SPACE

A whole new world of additive sculpture has opened up with the growing utilization of materials such as reed, drinking straws, pick-up, paste and applicator sticks, tongue depressors, toothpicks, *found materials*, fast-drying glues, and metal adhesives. Whatever one may label these constructions, whether space modulator, stable, mobile, or assemblage, they definitely attract and hold the interest of today's space-conscious youngster and add a new, exciting dimension to the elementary art program.

The teacher's first consideration in the implementation of these construction projects is to see that sufficient materials are on hand. Adequate storage facilities for constructions in progress must also be planned. Round reed (numbers 3 and 4 are recommended), paste sticks, and fast-drying glue can be obtained from school or art supply companies; applicator sticks and tongue depressors from drug stores; and other items from grocery or department stores. A letter to the parents, including a list of *found materials* especially useful in 3-D constructions, might build a store of discards and scraps that would get the project started (see Appendix E for suggestions).

OPPOSITE PAGE—Photography by Dr. W. Robert Nix, University of Georgia, Athens. THIS PAGE—Three-dimensional constructions in reed and construction paper. Grade 5, Iowa City, Iowa. Grade 6, Milwaukee Public Schools.

In reed constructions an orientation session is recommended in which the children can practice with the material to discover its limitations and possibilities. They will learn that they can bend the reed but that it also has a breaking point. In reed projects where many curved or circular elements are required, the reed should be presoaked in water a day in advance so it will be very pliable during construction. A good surface on which to construct curved reed shapes is a piece of Celotex or acoustic tile. A piece of corrugated cardboard may also be used but is not as effective. A demonstration by the teacher to clarify the reed-bending process is suggested. Cut moist reed with wire cutter or tinsnips to sizes desired. Bend to shape and pin securely to Celotex or cardboard base criss-crossing the pins on both sides of the reed to keep it from springing out of shape. For spiral shapes the moist reed can be wound around a large wood dowel or a cardboard tube and secured with gum tape or staples until dry.

The reed must be thoroughly dry before glue or cement is applied to seal joints. An overnight drying period is recommended. An extra-fast drying cement such as Testor's Formula AA or Sig-ment is suggested. Allow sufficient time for the glue to dry before removing holding pins.

These reed constructions began with sketches of fish during a field trip to natural museum. Grades 5 and 6, Iowa City, Iowa.

194

✳ If the subject of the reed construction is an animal, bird, fish, insect, or human figure, a preliminary line drawing is often helpful in establishing the basic form. As the construction grows, the unique possibilities and limitations of the materials themselves will make adaptations and adjustments in the design necessary. This is part of the challenge and excitement of additive sculpture.

In many instances the children will want to create nonobjective, abstract, or geometrically-orchestrated constructions allowing the materials to dictate the form. This is particularly true when straws, sticks, and toothpicks are the medium. The design grows stick by stick, straw by straw, pick by pick.

Unless the construction itself has a stable footing, it is advisable that an auxiliary base of wood, plywood, or Masonite be utilized. A painted cigar box makes a satisfactory base. If necessary, it can be weighted with sand and sealed with tape to stabilize it. Determine the number and the placement of the supports required, then drill or punch small holes into the base at these points. Begin the structure by inserting and gluing the first sections of reed, sticks, toothpicks, or straws into these holes. The number of these supports or underpinnings will vary depending on the complexity and size of the structure.

There is a wealth of inexpensive constructing materials that includes waste products and found materials for students to experiment with in their space adventures. Here youngsters explore the possibilities of packing paper and plastic packing pieces, of metal filter discards, scrap wood, and straws, and assorted items.

The students and teacher will discover, too, a host of affinitive materials to enrich or embellish the reed or stick constructions. Many of these will be *found objects* such as bottle corks, thread spools, wood clothes pins, balsa wood strips, string, wood beads, pegs and buttons, round fishing corks, ping pong balls, pegboard scraps, small rubber balls, wood picnic spoons, colored tissue and construction paper, and cardboard rings from Scotch tape dispensers.

The completed constructions may be given a coat of spray paint if desired. Black or white is especially effective in unifying different parts of the structure and creating a strong, visual impact.

There are many avenues open to the youngster who wishes to explore the possibilities of constructive or additive sculpture. Wire sculpture has a special appeal to boys. Wire can be combined with *found metal objects* to create exciting three-dimensional inventions. Toothpick and applicator stick constructions can be coated with or dipped into melted crayon or wet plaster. Wooden picnic spoons can be assembled into a unique sculpture of their own. Corrugated cardboard can be cut into various-sized shapes then slotted and glued together into a stabile. Cardboard mailing tubes can be cut into various-sized cylinders and circles then assembled into animals, insects, and figures. It is recommended that a vibrating jig saw (Dremel) be used to cut heavy cardboard or cardboard tubes.

Wood scraps, tattered rope, straw, dried corn husks, wire, string, newspapers, discarded screening or metal lathe—all these can be exploited in today's school art program. On this and opposite page examples from Japanese elementary schools.

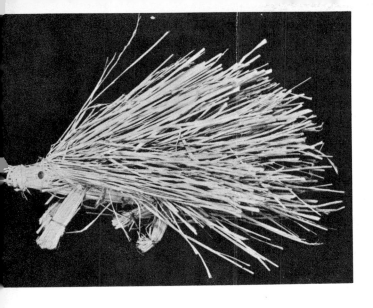

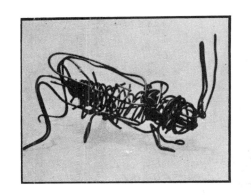

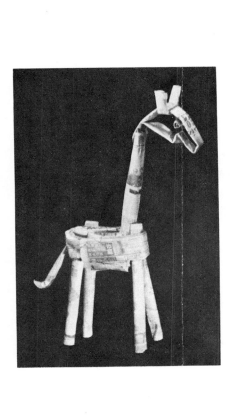

197

BOX SCULPTURE

Older children often need a change of pace sparked by new challenges, new materials, and new techniques to keep them interested in art. Imaginative construction utilizing cardboard boxes, mailing tubes, and assorted *found objects* give upper-grade youngsters a rare opportunity to express their individual ideas in a unique three-dimensional form, to recycle discarded materials into new configurations, to struggle with a problem of intricate construction until it is resolved, and to prove the old adage once more that "the whole is greater than the sum of its parts" in a truly creative way.

At least 2 to 4 weeks before the project begins, the children should be reminded to start collecting discarded boxes of all sizes and shapes from grocery, drug, shoe, and department stores. This early personal involvement on the part of the youngsters builds high interest in the project ahead.

All the accumulated boxes and *found objects* can be stored until needed in a large cardboard carton or, if desired, each child could keep his or her own collection of items in a strong paper shopping bag labeled with the child's name.

This "monster" was created out of discarded boxes, corrugated paper, pick-up sticks, wooden clothespins, mailing tubes, and magazine ads. Grade 4, Iowa City, Iowa.

Tools, equipment, and special materials that can contribute to the success of the project include straight pins, masking tape, paper clips, string, double-faced tape, rubber bands, gum tape, coping saw, vibrating jig saw (optional), white liquid glue, rubber cement, school paste, scissors, paper punch, nails, old magazines, and coloring materials. X-acto knives and single-edge razor blades (preferably in holders) are essential for cutting holes in the cardboard boxes but they must be handled with caution under teacher supervision.

Several problems unique to this project should be resolved before the class begins the actual box constructions. These include adequate storage for the *found objects* and for the constructions in progress as well as a sufficient supply of fastening equipment and materials.

Imaginative themes for these constructions are almost limitless: spacemen, space stations and ships, robots, creatures from another planet, toys, rockets, homes and vehicles of the future, fantastic designs for playground equipment, and purely nonobjective space modulators.

One method of initiating the project is to ask the children to select three or four different-sized boxes or tubes from the general supply or from their individual collections and manipulate these into various juxtapositions until some arrangement or structure triggers a subject idea. After the youngsters decide on the basic shape of their creation, they may want

to make some sketches to help them with their construction, although such sketches are optional. The real excitement develops as the youngster sees the construction grow and change as new materials are found and added. What began conceptually as a "Home of the Future" might easily emerge in the final stages as "A Creature from Another Planet."

The most difficult part of this project is the mechanics involved in fastening the separate boxes together and securing the appendages to the main structure. Some recommended approaches follow: Glue then tie the boxes together with string or cord until the glue dries; fasten the boxes together with a ribbon of masking tape that goes around both boxes; in many instances the glue should dry overnight for a strong weld.

When mailing tubes or cardboard cylinders are used as appendages or box joiners, be sure the hole cut for the tube insertion is slightly smaller than the tube itself. This will generally provide a tight, stable joint; for real security, liquid glue can be applied around the insertion. In some cases the teacher will have to help the children in cutting the holes into thick, resistant cardboard.

In the construction of standing monsters, spacemen, or other fantastic creatures, the problem of making the figure stand upright must be resolved. If necessary, a third leg or support should be created. Sometimes a tail can be added for balance, sometimes the arms can hold gear that touches the ground for a stabilizer.

200

More creative box sculpture employing among other things egg cartons, paper cups, wooden beads and pegs, thumbtack boxes, corks, and discarded ping pong balls. Grade 5, Iowa City, Iowa.

Interest in the project may be renewed by suggesting further implementation with other *found materials* for textural or decorative delineation. Encourage the children to exploit egg cartons, corrugated cardboard, paper drinking straws, plastic packing noodles, round wooden clothespins, plain and colored toothpicks, paste sticks, dowel rods, corks, wooden beads, ping pong balls, and game pieces. Some of these materials may be purchased in quantities at little cost from discount houses or school supply firms.

The outcome of this project depends in great part on the number and variety of boxes and other *found items* gathered by students and teacher. Sometimes an unusual box turns up that is just right for the head of a monster and provides the inspiration for the rest of the construction. Often a box can be partially opened and hinged to become the mouth and jaws of an animal.

A decision must be made, too, on whether to paint the completed box construction or leave it as it is. In some instances, the raw containers with their printed designs are so colorful and exciting that painting them would only detract from their expressive and unique quality. However, in cases where the sculpture is not painted, the characteristic features that give the creature or figure its individuality must be emphasized, especially the eyes, ears, nose, and mouth.

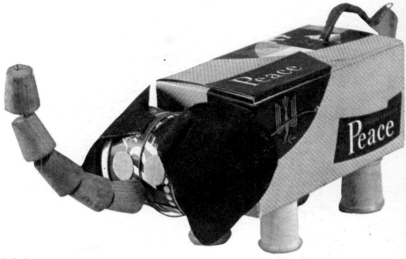

Let the shape of the box itself trigger the student's imagination. It can also provide some of the decorative effects. Square and rectangular boxes as exploited in the ship are easier for primary children to assemble. It is not always necessary to paint box sculpture. The elephant has a cork trunk and discarded thread spools for legs. Grades 4 and 5, Japan.

201

If the constructions are to be painted, certain factors will have to be taken into consideration. The glossy surfaces of many boxes will resist tempera or watercolor paints. Soap will have to be added to the paint to make it adhere. Latex paint covers all surfaces effectively. If cost is not a factor, spray paint is recommended. Apply in a well-ventilated area or out of doors.

Another possibility is to cover or mask the distracting parts of the boxes by camouflaging them with a collage treatment of colored construction paper, newspaper, comic book sheets, colored tissue paper, magazine cut-outs, wallpaper samples, or discarded decorative wrapping and gift papers.

There are endlessly exciting possibilities in *box and found object sculpture*. The teacher and students who are resourceful enough, curious enough, and brave enough to try it have a real "adventure in art" awaiting them.

MASKS

Mask making in the elementary schools has always been a popular activity but unfortunately one in which the design considerations have seldom been fully understood or effectively implemented. Too often compositional factors involving the mask authentic have been minimized and colors applied in a haphazard, form-negating manner.

The most exciting, the most striking masks through the centuries have almost always been based on an abstract, stylized concept rather than on natural appearances, and often on a basic format which utilized broad, economical, and simple shapes such as the oval, the circle, the ellipse, or a combination of these. Masks of various ethnological and primitive cultures owe their impact to a pure and semisymmetrical version of the face, whether of man or animal.

LEFT—Construction-paper masks. The three-dimensional character is created by cutting slits into a 12″ x 18″ sheet of colored construction paper and stapling into a rounded form. Grade 4. TOP—Preliminary pen and ink drawings for a mask project. Grade 6.

204

Although very young children can, on occasion, create simple, expressively naïve masks if effectively motivated, mask making, because of its symbolic connotations, traditional overtones, and often complex techniques, should usually be postponed until youngsters reach the upper elementary grades.

A study of masks by tribal Africans and North Pacific Coast Indians, among others, reveals certain significant and recurring aspects. Facial features that capture mood or spirit are emphasized or exaggerated. Characteristic elements of a face are never minimized or distorted to appear as something they are not, such as the asterisk-shaped eyes or mouth that are found in stereotyped versions.

The best masks are imbued with the essence of a particular mood: astonishment, serenity, power, anger, dignity, reverence, joy, fury, peace, frenzy, despair, or innocence. A continuity of forms and features, as exemplified by the movement of the nose structure into the eyebrow contour, is a major characteristic in primitive masks.

ABOVE—Construction paper and yarn. Grade 3, Japan. TOP RIGHT—Mexican festival mask. BOTTOM—Masks made from corner sections of grocery cartons and painted with tempera. Grade 4, Barrow Elementary School, Athens, Georgia.

205

Facial decoration can be effectively employed to heighten the visual quality of a mask. Students may use lines that repeat and emphasize dominant features, lines to create pattern or texture on the face, or lines that delineate the hair or beard. Color should be used judiciously since it can either enhance or jeopardize the mask's impact. It must be integrated with the features, not superficially applied, and must emphasize rather than negate the mask's dominant characteristics. Subtle and limited color schemes and combinations should be encouraged. The primary colors should be used with discretion, although they may be effectively employed to provide a necessary contrast.

The incentive for mask making could spring just as naturally from a social studies unit as it does from overworked Halloween themes. Children should be challenged to create masks as art forms in themselves.

Materials and processes that lead to qualitative mask making are in a sense limited. Papier-mâché over a clay base or mold is still the most effectively controlled technique allowing for highly individual interpretations and for delicate facial modeling. Also recommended is papier-mâché or plaster-impregnated gauze applied over a *found object* or kitchen utensil such as a mixing bowl, round plastic dishpan or salad bowl, or a beach ball. As the form develops, it can be embellished with additional pieces of styrofoam, bent cardboard, and *found objects* to create nose, eye, mouth, and ear shapes and with string, yarn, or raffia for hair, beard, and other textures. These details are

206

TOP—Mask carved from wood. Used in classical Japanese Nô drama. CENTER—Mask made of construction paper and magazine ads. Grade 6, Barnett Shoals Elementary School, Athens, Georgia. BOTTOM—The painted face as a mask. Courtesy of Dr. Jack Stoops.

covered with a final layer of gauze or paper toweling and then the entire mask is painted if desired.

A popular mask-making technique is the paper-sculpture method, but it often requires intricate cutting and scoring of paper to achieve effective three-dimensional features. It has many possibilities, however, and can be pursued in the ordinary classroom because of the availability of materials and tools. It is recommended that a period of exploration be scheduled to discover the 3-D potential of paper before embarking on the mask project itself.

For children in the primary grades the creation of a paper plate, paper sack, or totem-pole mask is the most practical approach since it does not involve a complex three-dimensional technique. A study of early American Indian life provides rich motivation for many art projects, including the construction of a totem pole by the class as a whole.

To begin with, each child chooses a sheet of 12 by 18 inch colored construction paper as the background for his totem mask. Placing the paper horizontally on his desk with the larger border at the bottom, he draws his mask with white chalk in the center of the paper. The larger he draws it the better. The top and bottom of his mask can touch the papers edge if he wishes. Following the custom of the Indian totem carvers, he can make his mask that of an animal, bird, medicine man, or whatever he desires.

LEFT—Playsacks designed for Creative Playthings, Princeton, New Jersey, by Fredun Shapur. RIGHT—Children of Athens Academy, Athens, Georgia designed their own Halloween "trick or treat" costumes. Grade 1.

When he completes his drawing, he may color his mask in several ways: he can paint it with tempera; he can paste colored paper or cloth over it; he can color it with crayon or oil pastels. He should be encouraged to exploit unusual colors in his mask, to repeat colors for unity, to create contrast by juxtaposing light and dark colors, and to make important parts of the mask dominant through use of vivid colors.

When the mask is completed, parts of it may be made three-dimensional by cutting slits with a single-edge razor blade around one side or more of an eye, nose, mouth, or ear and folding these outward from the main mask. The child may also add supplemental pieces for teeth, fangs, horns, earrings, and eyebrows.

There are several methods of making totem poles out of the construction-paper masks. A recommended technique is to begin with an empty gallon tin food container from the cafeteria. Weight it with sand. Wrap a large sheet of plain or colored tagboard around it, fastening the sheet securely into a cylinder with strong tape. Apply glue where the paper overlaps. Build another tagboard cylinder above the first if desired. Repeat until the height needed is reached. With the tagboard cylinder as a sturdy base, fasten the masks around it with glue, stapler, masking tape, or gun tacker. Once the basic totem cylinder is constructed, the youngsters may embellish it with additional wings, feet, and arms made out of painted cardboard.

208

Masks designed for a totem pole. 12″ x 18″ colored construction paper and oil pastel were the materials. The completed masks were taped around discarded food tins from the school cafeteria. They could also be mounted on or tacked to a hanging wood strip or lath. Eyes, ears, noses, and mouths can be slit open and bent back for a 3-D effect.

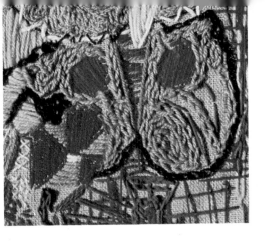

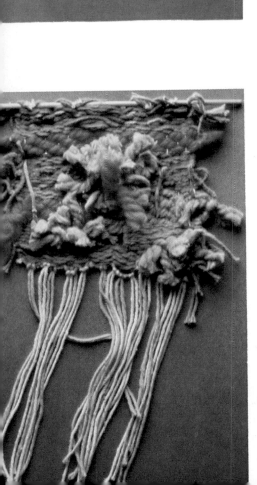

LEFT COLUMN—Expressive weaving. Grade 5, Lawton Elementary School, Ann Arbor, Michigan. CENTER COLUMN—Stitchery on burlap. Pattie Hillsman School, Athens, Georgia. RIGHT COLUMN—Group project stitchery. Theme: "Snakes in Their Habitats." Oconee County Elementary School, Georgia.

"Which is Earth? No. 57." Ink and acrylic with collage on paper. Liu Kuo-Sung, 1970, 33 1/2" x 23 1/4".

7

FUNDAMENTALS OF ART

The teacher of art in the elementary school today is often handicapped by a limited background in art fundamentals. A share of the blame for this deficiency must rest with the college or university art education instructor who allows the students to compromise, to settle for less than they are capable of achieving in art, and who permits them to dissipate valuable time and energy in instant activities that call for little more than hand-and-eye dexterity or step-by-step manipulation of tools and materials such as pull-the-string effects, ink blots, folded snow-flake cut outs, or pre-school fingerpainting exercises. Another disservice is furnished the interning young teachers by the instructor who encourages them to create in a child-like idiom with child-oriented subject matter so that what often emerges in so many college art education courses are coy rabbits, candy-colored elves, puppies, and baby pandas, everything in fact except the personal, mature, and immediate experiences of the students themselves.

The qualitative, exemplary elementary-art-methods course, whether geared to the classroom teacher or the special art teacher, should provide the student with significant high-caliber *art doing* and *art appreciating* experiences. Fundamentally valid art concepts and principles, based on recurring compositional factors in the visual arts, both past and present, should color and permeate the college or university art-education program. Its content should be characterized by a deliberate and continuing emphasis on individual and expressive drawing. Preliminary drawings or sketches should be the rule rather than the exception in the majority of studio projects. In essence, the student's inquisitive investigation of his environment, his continuous experimentation with new materials and new techniques, his multisensual perceptual development, his self-identification with the natural order, and his individual, imaginative potential should be identified, encouraged, and rewarded at every possible stage.

This chapter, like Chapter 3 "The Teacher's Role," is illustrated with the creative efforts of college and university students preparing to be teachers and with the work of artist-teachers. ABOVE—Future classroom teacher exploring the use of yarn as a collage material. The theme: "Portrait of a Classmate."

Teachers of art in our elementary schools can grow professionally if they "keep in touch" by reviewing and studying the increasing number of fine publications on art and artists. As they read and catalog the contemporary reports on design, composition, and structure, they will discover recurring references to the basic elements of art: point, line, shape, color, value, pattern, texture, form, and space. They will also find repeated references to art's fundamental principles or laws: balance, rhythm-repetition, variety, emphasis, dominance, subordination, radiation, and unity. Art, they gradually discover, is a continuously challenging journey, a constantly changing adventure with relatively few shortcuts to successful composition or good design, and although they may borrow ideas and inspiration from the rich past, they must re-interpret their findings in the context of the present. The future demands new approaches, new strategies, and new techniques it is true, yet there are some important guideposts, some avenues to design and composition which teachers can turn to in their search for a teaching strategy so that they may with confidence help the children in the art class who rely on them.

A primary concern of teachers of elementary art should be an understanding and implementation of the *linear image*. The line drawing is the basic structural system of all graphic composition. Expressive, sensitively drawn lines usually vary in pressure, width, or emphasis. They can be delicate, bold, flowing, static, rhythmic, awkward, violent, or dynamic.

ESPAÑA "Color intaglio, Mauricio Lasansky, 1956, 32" x 21".

They are achieved on occasion through freedom or spontaneity and, in other instances, through thoughtful and deliberate action. They may converge, radiate, meander, or intercept one another to create interest, impact, tension, or chaos. An object, motif, or image is visually more exciting when delineated in a variety of sensitive lines. Lines expressively drawn can create and define shapes, values, and paths of motion. We can turn to nature and man-made objects as sources of line variety: frost, tree branches, spider webs, water ripples, veins in leaves, sea weed, wood grain, skeletons, bark of trees, insect wings, bird cages, kite lines, bicycle-wheel spokes, bridge spans, jet streams, road maps, telephone and power lines, and TV antennas. Children in school should be afforded many opportunities to explore the possibilities of line with its myriad interpretations.

A study of pictorial design, of composition in painting, eventually centers on the *shape* of things. The shapes created by lines merging, intersecting, or touching each other take many forms. They may be square, rectangular, complex, round, oval, cellular, or amorphous. Shape can also be created in design by other means such as color washes, smudging, flowing ink, object printing, paper cutting, and assorted techniques. The achievement of varied, expressive shapes in a composition provides youngsters with one of art's greatest challenges.

Nature is the richest source of inspiration for a study of variety of shapes. Natural forms and shapes like those found in a tree branch, a leaf, a sea shell,

a cell, a pebble, a petal, or a feather are usually much more varied, more subtle than those based on mathematical formulas. Perhaps this is the reason landscape artists have often turned to dilapidated, aging buildings as inspiration for their compositions instead of the clean and coldly geometric shapes of contemporary architecture. There is an illusive quality inherent in old things that gives them a special magic in the artist's eyes. To clarify this point, consider a utilitarian object such as a window blind. For purposes of function the slots in a blind must have similar dimensions and be spaced equally. But when a contemporary artist draws the window blind as part of a composition, he invariably changes the measured perfection of the rectangular slots to achieve more variety in shape against shape. He may alter the direction of the slots, he may omit some, he may add others. He is using the artist's license to visually interpret the object in a more personal, more expressive way.

There is far too much reliance in art classes on geometric formula and mathematical perfection in the rendition of table tops, cabinets, doors, windows, building façades, fences, sidewalks, and other utilitarian structures. Both teacher and students should turn more often to a contemplation of nature's varied forms when their own inventiveness in creating interesting shapes needs re-charging.

The shapes of things or objects such as trees, animals, houses, vehicles, and people in a composition are sometimes called *positive* shapes or spaces. The areas around them are often referred to as *negative* shapes or spaces, even though the negative space may include something definite such as sky, ground, or water. In any case, where the *positive shapes* are varied in size and shape, the *negative space* is usually more varied and interesting. When a composition is effectively varied, it is usually *in good shape*.

Value and the contrast produced by juxtaposing a variety of values play an important role in pictorial design. *Value,* simply stated, refers to the light and dark elements in a composition. Every shade (darkness) and tint (lightness) of every color has a place on the value scale. Teachers and students must learn to see color in terms of its value in order to create effective and exciting color contrasts. Value analyses of famous paintings can help students understand effective dark and light orchestration and juxtaposition. Compositions with sharply contrasting values are usually dramatic and dynamic in theme. Less contrasting value relationships provide a tranquil, calm, and sometimes a more unified interpretation. Value can be utilized also to create movement in a painting and lead the viewer from one part of the picture to another.

Color in painting is a continuing challenge to art students, to teachers of art, and, often, to professional artists. It is not uncommon to see an art student perform with confidence when he draws or composes in black and white, yet find himself completely frustrated when he tackles color. All the color theories, color wheels, and color schemes offered to date cannot help him, it seems, in his dilemma. The academic formulas no longer hold. For example, what were once identified as receding colors may now prove advancing colors. Colors that simply "did not go together" according to traditionalists of the "thirties" now are juxtaposed audaciously. Artists Henri Matisse, Pablo Picasso, and Hans Hofmann are acclaimed pioneers in liberating painting from local color renditions and restrictions. *Today anything goes in color—if it succeeds!*

To the elementary teacher of art this state of affairs may suggest chaos and confusion in the realm of color orientation and color expression. Not to worry! There are some concepts, some practices that can lead students to an understanding of color, to its limitations and its possibilities.

In most colleges and universities art instructors suggest a palette of colors for their students, and although this palette may vary, it is similar in one respect—it is usually a limited color palette.

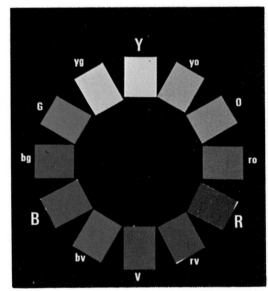

Today's color explorations open exciting avenues for both teacher and student. The new day-glo and black light colors, together with the psychedelic color implications, tempt the youngster to try the unusual, the innovative. A study of the color wheel and color harmonies can help if applied wisely.

215

Limitation, plays an important role in the mastery of color composition. Sometimes the art student is advised to limit his palette to black, white, gray, and one primary or secondary color, or to all the tints and shades of a single color as for example in a monochromatic scheme. A more complex, yet controlled, orchestration involves the use of analogous colors, those adjacent to each other on the color wheel.

To avoid the pitfalls of clashing colors and student chromatic relationships, many art instructors recommend minimizing the intensity of colors used in a composition. This process, sometimes referred to as neutralization or dulling of a color, involves the mixing of complementary colors, those opposite each other on the color wheel. Many colors now available in oil pastels, crayon, tempera, polymer, or oil are already neutralized; for example, sienna, umber, ochre, brown, earth green, and sepia.

Another strategy recommended by painting instructors to give unity or coherence to a painting is to mix a miniscule amount of a selected color with every other color used in the composition. This is in essence another kind of neutralization. Still another avenue to unity in color manipulation is glazing. Complementary colors diluted with the recommended solvents are applied over the initial high key colors to neutralize them. This is a highly technical procedure and must be handled sensitively. Some designated oil paints are specifically used as glazing colors.

Even though many of the standard color theories have been questioned and even discarded, some suc-cessful strategies in color usage persist. A fraction of bright, intense color goes a long way in a chromatic composition that is basically neutral or soft-keyed. Colors may be repeated to create movement and unity, but it is recommended that size and shape of the repeated color be varied. Dark or cool colors usually recede; bright or warm colors generally advance. Complementary colors such as red and green in their fullest intensities create vibrant contrasts when juxtaposed. Black, white, and gray can be combined with any color scheme without creating any tangible color conflicts. Often, as in the case of black accents, they may add the sparkle of sharp definition to a color design. Both teacher and student must always be aware that the character and impact of a color depends greatly on the colors surrounding it; for example, a green shape on a blue-green background may be relatively unnoticed, but intense orange against an intense blue background will vibrate and arrest the eye.

The painters of the post-impressionistic and expressionistic era, including Wassily Kandinsky, Franz Marc, Karl Schmidt-Rottluff and Odilon Redon, not to mention contemporary colorists such as Josef Albers, Mark Rothko, and Paul Jenkins, have provided the art world with a whole new approach to color. No longer do artists rely on the use of local color which only captures the natural or surface appearance of things. A more personal, more subjective interpretation of color in its many aspects is the painter's goal now with resulting surprises such as blue horses, purple turtles, and green people. Painting today takes on a new exciting reality with an imaginative use of color.

Teachers who wish to learn more about color and its expressive possibilities should study the paintings of the impressionists, post-impressionists, and abstract expressionists as well as the diverse, exciting, and sometimes shocking color manifestations of today. They should turn, too, for inspiration in using color to the luminous stained glass windows of Gothic cathedrals, to the jewel-like miniatures of ancient India and Persia, to the shimmering mosaics of Byzantium, and to the fascinating *ukiyoe* color woodcuts of Japan.

Space as an element in composition and design can often confuse the young student. In two-dimensional expression, space is sometimes designated as the empty or negative areas between objects or positive forms. This kind of space is commonly referred to as decorative or flat space. Another category of space to be considered is space-in-depth, often described as plastic space. Common pictorial devices for achieving the illusion of space-in-depth on a two-dimensional plane as in a painting are diminishing sizes of objects, sharp and clear details in foreground, with blurred, indistinct elements in the background, overlapping of shapes or forms, intense colors in foreground with neutral or dulled colors in background, and the effective utilization of traditional perspective principles such as vanishing points, horizon levels, and converging lines.

The elementary art teacher will discover that decorative exploitation of space is a natural expression for young children. The more objects or details they include in their pictures, the more intricate, varied, and exciting their nonobject space becomes. As the children grow older, they discover other aspects of creating pictorial space through tension, foreshortening, and shading. Some of this feeling for space comes intuitively, but many children must be taught the intricacies of perspective and space-in-depth. Neither laws nor rules of perspective should be imposed on a child unless he indicates a need for them. Students cannot insure the success of a painting by following the canons of perspective. Much too often a dependence on perspective formulas has lead to sterility in composition. The same compositional pitfall awaits the student who relies too rigidly on natural lighting and on shadows or reflections to create solid forms on a two-dimensional plane. Teachers should encourage their students to explore visual interpretations other than those based solely on natural laws and effects.

Another avenue to successful picture making is the effective exploitation of *balance* or *symmetry*. Teachers and students should be familiar with the two types of balance: symmetrical or formal and asymmetrical or informal. Although formal balance was commonly used in many Renaissance paintings, the modern and contemporary artist has for the most part eschewed the rigid, static formulas of symmetrical juxtaposition. Purely formal compositions, where objects on

217

the right balance similar objects on the left, usually lack the open-ended orchestration and variety which encourages the viewer to look at a painting creatively, each time discovering some new avenue of approach to its appreciation, some subtle emphasis, or some hidden beauty.

A common misconception about composition in art is that *emphasis* can be achieved by making something very large and putting it in the center of the picture. Size and placement in the composition by themselves do not insure domination. Other factors must be considered. If the motif or figure in the middle of the picture is simple in form, subdued in color, lacking in detail, pattern, or texture and surrounded by brighter elements, then in all probability it will attract no more attention than a similarly treated object on the periphery of the composition. To achieve emphasis in a picture an object must have other attributes than centricity itself. It must, in fact, have eccentricity.

Despite the reminder that there are no hard and fast rules in composition, teachers and students usually discover that pictorial design is much more successful, has more flexibility, more fluidity, when the principle subject or figure is not placed exactly in the center of the composition or page. As we study the works of contemporary painters, printmakers, and collagists, we are often made aware of the subtle and psychological utilization of asymmetry these artists

218

Disintegrating, weathered buildings, like aging men and women, often reveal visual form that artists respond to. Here author Ted Ramsay captures the "hidden" aesthetic components in a tenement alley. Note the variety of line and pattern in the drawing and how subtle the changes in the resulting collage.

employ. Although, at first glance, the key figure or shape appears formally centered, a closer investigation indicates an ingenuous shift off-center. In some instances where the central object dominates the composition, as in a flower study or figure portrait, the break-up of negative space on each side of the central axis is so varied that centricity poses no handicap.

Variety and diversity in composition have always played a significant role in the history of the visual arts. A study of the recurring aspects of variety within unity in great works of art, past and present, will be of inestimable value to the teacher of elementary art. Analyses of masterpieces of drawing, painting, and printmaking reveal the artist's reliance on and constant utilization of a variety of shapes and forms. Seldom does one discover two shapes in a composition that are exactly alike!

Nature's wonders and its everchanging elements can provide inspiration with multiple evidences of unusual variety: ice floes breaking up on a river, the branches of roots and trees, the crystals in snowflakes, the cells in a honeycomb, the cracks in mud flats, oil flowing on water, erosion in soil, snowdrift swirls, and patterns of clouds. Though man is nature's child, he must learn to employ subtle variety in his creative imagery. Too often the shapes he makes or invents are monotonous, mathematically restrictive, sadly conventional, and stereotyped. He might do well to look once more and intently at the wings of a butterfly, the stripes on a zebra, the spots on a leopard, the feathers of a bird, the scales of a fish, or the frost on a windowpane.

Note the use of asymmetry in these figure compositions made in author's classes at Georgia by students preparing to be art teachers. Class models were employed in the tissue collage (center), and multicrayon engraving (right). The tempera batik (left) juxtaposes two figures in an off-center yet harmonious balance.

Variety as a force in pictorial design can be exploited in many ways and on many occasions. It can be applied to every element in a composition—line, shape, value, color, pattern, texture—to give excitement and power to a painting, but it must be used discriminatively and counterbalanced by a repetition of these same art elements if unity is to be achieved. Emphasis, too, must be considered, and also subordination. The principle of variety can help students in the placement of objects, figures, or shapes in their compositions—these may begin on different levels, stop at different heights, overlap each other to create different shapes, different negative spaces between them.

The unified composition in which diverse lines, shapes, colors, values, and textures are incorporated or fused in an ordered and satisfying way should be the goal of teachers and students in elementary art. In too many instances, objects and figures are isolated in space, treated as separate vignettes. Too often the figure, vase, animal, tree, or house is lost in the middle of the page with no indication of spatial or environmental relationship. This pictorial limitation can often be redeemed by the use of subordinate or overlapping shapes, through the repetition of the object or figure in varied sizes and positions, through the utilization of related or complementary backgrounds, or through the employment of environmental aspects that relate to the central theme.

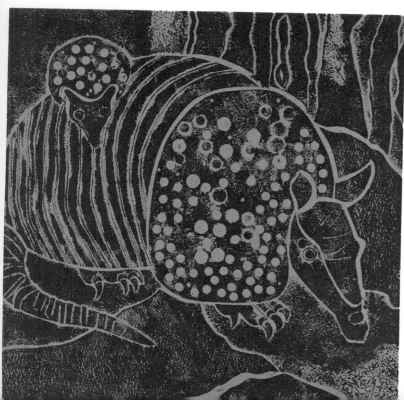

220

TOP—Lino print over newspaper section. Another example of effective asymmetry. To retain clarity in the print, avoid printing over backgrounds that are too dark especially where the light and dark pattern is important. BOTTOM—Collograph, 12" x 12". Because of inking problems the size of the plates should be limited in large classes.

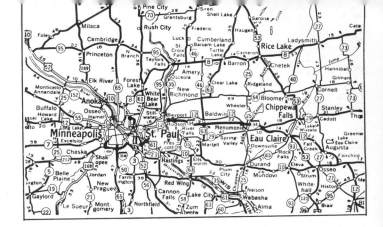

One effective method of achieving variety within unity in a composition and of breaking up the picture plane in a successful manner is to use the inspiration provided by a road map. Roads on maps, in most instances, follow the natural contours and delineations of land and waterways, so they are excellent examples of variety in line and movement. In a map, as in a good composition, the eye moves (directionally) along the major highways or arterials with subordinate ventures along country roads. The areas created by connecting and bisecting routes on a map can be compared in many instances to the varied, amorphic shapes found in abstract or nonobjective paintings. The observer enters the painting (map) at one of the many possible inroads, then is led to a major interstate highway that carries him to a point of emphasis or center of interest (large city). Other subordinate roads (lines) radiate, disperse, or branch from this focal spot to less important areas of emphasis (small towns and suburbs). The more complex the painting, the more avenues in and out of the composition are provided giving the observer an opportunity to choose a different approach or entry each time he comes to view the painting.

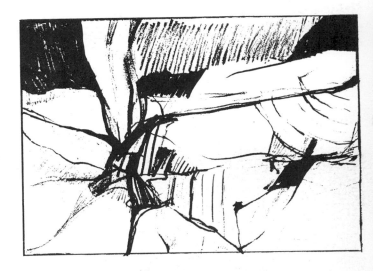

TOP—A bird's eye view of the city. Upper-grade youngster, West Germany. Courtesy of The Pelikan Company. RIGHT —One interpretation of the road map analogy. TOP RIGHT—The map. CENTER—The resultant sketch. BOTTOM—The color orchestration. Note again the asymmetrical composition.

221

In this age of jets, rockets, computers, and moon landings it is indeed difficult for youngsters not to be caught up in the hectic rush of events. Perhaps that is the reason why so many art students race through their work and why facile, instant, minimal painting appeals to them. Too much of what we see in art today reveals a lack of purpose, of serious effort, and of patient skill. We are misled if we equate speed of execution with freedom of expression. A spontaneous, fresh quality in a work of art is achieved usually after much practice and deliberation. It is the result of many hours, many years of mastering a skill or technique, of developing visual awareness, and of integrating mind, heart, eye, and hand. The basic art principles documented and reviewed in this chapter are not a *new and improved* formula, but if used wisely they can provide the elementary teacher of art with a realistic, workable art foundation on which to build a qualitative program. There will always be exceptions to the rule, but in most cases and in most classrooms, a fundamentals approach, based on a sound understanding and implementation of art's recurring elements and laws, will prove to be the most stabilizing and significant.

TOP—Cloth, yarn, and thread can also function as the artist's palette. Foster Marlow, San Marcos, Texas proves it in this beautifully crafted stitchery-appliqué. BOTTOM— "Aftermath" is by author Frank Wachowiak who employs a bold black outline to give impact to the colors.

222

A

CHILDREN: THEIR CHARACTERISTICS

FIRST AND SECOND GRADERS

Are rather active and easily excited
Like to work with their hands
Have a strong feeling of possessiveness
Are eager to learn
Want to be first
Have a limited span of interest
Are easily fatigued
Take great pride in their work
Are usually gregarious
Have feelings that are easily hurt
Are alternately cooperative and uncooperative
Can usually grasp only one idea at a time
Delight in imaginative games, stories, and plays
Want the approval of classmates and teacher
Still live in their own secret world
Are interested in new things to touch and taste

TOP—Linoleum Print. Grade 3. BOTTOM—Children involved in painting are lost in their own world. Photo courtesy of Naomi Dietz, California State College, Fullerton, California.

223

FIRST AND SECOND GRADERS

Like to pretend and engage in make-believe
Are fascinated in moving and mechanical devices
Enjoy sports, television, holidays, illustrated
books, family outings, school field trips, new
clothes

THIRD AND FOURTH GRADERS

Have improved eye-hand coordination
Have better command of small muscles
Are becoming aware of differences in people
Begin to set standards for themselves
Are learning to be responsible, orderly, and
cooperative
Begin to form separate sex groups
May join gangs or cliques
Enjoy comic books and magazines
Are growing in self-evaluation and evaluation
of others
Are now able to concentrate for a longer period
of time
Are developing a growing interest in travel
Are interested in the life processes of plants and
animals
Are developing a sense of humor
Are avid hobbyists and collectors

FIFTH AND SIX GRADERS

Are developing a set of values, a sense of right
and wrong
Begin to concentrate more on individual interests
Are now more interested in activities that relate
to their sex groupings
Are becoming more dependable, responsible, and
reasonable
Are interested in doing things "right"
Develop interests outside of school—in their
community and in the world itself
Begin to criticize grown-ups and anyone in
authority
Are undergoing critical emotional and physical
changes
Vary in maturity. Girls are often more devel-
oped physically, emotionally, physiologically,
and mentally than boys
Build their interest in collections and hobbies
Begin a phase of hero-worship
Very often like to be by themselves, away from
adult interference
Are growing to be self-conscious and self-critical
Enjoy working in groups
Are developing an increasing interest-work span
Tend to form separate gangs or cliques accord-
ing to hobbies, interests, sex, neighborhoods

appendix

B

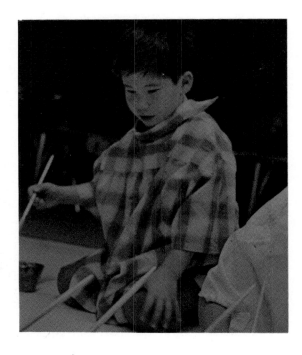

HOW CHILDREN GROW IN ART

Knowing what young children are like, what their special interests and needs may be, are important requisites for successful teaching, but a basic understanding of what children do *naturally* in art as they draw and paint is just as crucial to the essential encouragement of their creative growth. The children's graphic potential, the richness and complexity of their imagery, varies with the stages of their physical, mental, physiological, and sociological development. Some children may have had pre-school experiences in working with art materials; others may have had limited creative opportunities. Some youngsters may have developed a keen interest in some particular phase of their environment, for example, in horses, cars, trains, bikes, birds, rockets, insect, rock or shell collections, and their observations will often distinguish their art work from that of other children in class because of their eidetic and perceptual abilities. Since children express best what they know best and what they are most sensitive to, or affected by, it is often possible for the discerning teacher to discover through their art what they respond to in their environment and what their attitudes, values, and feelings about life may be.

TOP—Lino Print. Grade 5. BOTTOM—Youngsters make countless decisions in their art. It is a true growing experience. Fullerton, California.

FIRST GRADE CHILDREN

Continue to draw the geometrical symbols of circle, square, triangle, oval, and rectangle together with the lines which they used earlier but now change and enrich these symbols as they react to new experiences

Use a basic symbol, such as a circle, to depict varied visual images—the sun, a human or animal head, a table, a flower, a tree top, even a room

Devise many possible variations of a human figure, a house, a dog, a tree

Repeat the symbols that they have mastered, over and over again

Use combinations of symbols that are different from others in class

Simplify their representations and are not too concerned with details

Draw things as they know and feel them to be: the band of sky like a canopy at the top of the page, the sun that appears in the upper corner of almost every picture, the railroad tracks that do not converge, the eyes high in the head, the tree with a trunk twice as big to make it strong

Draw related objects such as house and tree on a base line which might be the bottom edge of the page or a line drawn horizontally above it

Use color in a personal or emotional context without regard to its local use or identification

SECOND GRADE CHILDREN

Use color more naturalistically in some instances but as a rule limit themselves to one green for all trees and leaves, one blue for the sky unless motivated to see more variety

Change slowly, subtly from geometric, symbolic interpretations to more specific characterization and delineation

Begin to use more details in their pictures—hair, ribbons, buttons, belt buckles, eyebrows, eye glasses, shoelaces, costume jewelry, fingernails, purses, patterns in clothes

Sometimes draw both the inside and outside of a place, a person, or object in an X-ray interpretation

May use a fold-over technique to show people on both sides of a street, people around a table or a swimming pool, or players on a baseball field. Often the youngsters turn their papers completely around as they draw

Use characteristic apparel and detail to distinguish sexes, such as skirts and long hair for girl, trousers and shirts for boys

Draw distant things the same size as those nearer them but place them higher on the page

Sometimes draw things as they know them rather than how they see them, for example, a table with four legs when only two legs are visible, a house with three sides when only one side is visible

THIRD AND FOURTH GRADE CHILDREN

Begin to draw and compose with more conscious, deliberate planning, striving for more realistic proportions

Begin to create space and depth through use of overlapping shapes

May now select and arrange objects to fulfill the compositional needs

May in some instances introduce the horizon line to show distant space

Now draw distant objects and figures smaller as well as higher on the page

Make repeated efforts to show action in their drawings of people and animals but are often handicapped by technical shortcomings, by their inability to master relative proportion and foreshortening

FIFTH AND SIXTH GRADE CHILDREN

Become increasingly critical of their drawing ability and often so discouraged with their efforts that they may lose interest in art class unless they are sympathetically guided, encouraged, and motivated

Develop a growing curiosity to experiment with varied materials, tools, and complex processes

Experiment with dark and light patterns, with a variety of textural effects

Begin to use rudimentary perspective principles in drawing landscapes, buildings, streets, sidewalks, train tracks, fences, and roads

Choose subject matter for their art expression which relates to human interest and activities, to community and world events, and to current projects in ecology and space exploration

Become more interested in their environment as a source for their drawings and paintings

Sometimes attempt shading techniques to make drawn forms appear solid, cylindrical, and realistic

appendix

C

RECOMMENDED READINGS

BOOKS FOR CHILDREN

The letter following each book indicates whether it is suitable for the primary child (P), the upper-grade child (U), or children at either level (A).

Ames, Gerald, and Wyler, Rose. *Giant Golden Book of Biology.* New York: Golden Press, Inc., 1961. (U)

Bate, Norman. *When Cavemen Painted.* New York: Charles Scribner's Sons, 1963. (A)

Baumann, Hans. *The Caves of the Great Hunters.* New York: Pantheon Books, Inc., 1954. (U)

Borten, Helen. *Do You See What I See?* New York: Simon & Schuster, Inc., 1951. (P)

Branley, Franklyn M. *The Mystery of Stonehenge.* New York: Thomas Y. Crowell Company, 1969. (U)

Brodatz, Phil. *Textures.* New York: Dover Publications, Inc., 1967. (U)

Browner, Richard. *Look Again!* New York: Atheneum Publishers, 1962. (P)

Busch, Phyllis S. *Lions in the Grass.* Cleveland: The World Publishing Company, 1968. (P)

Chase, Alice Elizabeth. *Famous Paintings.* New York: Platt and Munk, 1962. (U)

Deny, Norman, and Josephine Filmer-Sankey. *The Bayeux Tapestry.* New York: Atheneum Publishers, 1966. (U)

TOP—Lino Print. Grade 5 The classroom teacher should make an effort to obtain some of these recommended books for children. The child who completes a project might be encouraged to read books on art and design.

Fenton, Carrol L., and Mildred A. Fenton. *In Prehistoric Seas*. Garden City, N.Y.: Doubleday & Company, Inc., 1963. (A)

Fisher, James. *Wonderful World of the Sea*. New York: Garden City Books, 1957. (U)

Gibson, Katharine. *Pictures to Grow Up With*. New York: Studio Publications, Inc., 1946. (A)

————. *More Pictures to Grow Up With*. New York: Studio Publications, Inc., 1946. (A)

————. *Pictures by Young Americans*. New York: Oxford University Press, Inc., 1946. (A)

Gill, Bob. *What Color is Your World?* New York: Ivan Obolensky, Inc., 1963. (A)

Gilliard, E. Thomas. *Living Birds of the World*. Garden City, N. Y.: Doubleday & Company, Inc., 1958. (A)

Glubok, Shirley. *The Art of Ancient Egypt*. New York: Atheneum Publishers, 1962. (U)

————. *The Art of Ancient Greece*. New York: Atheneum Publishers, 1963. (U)

————. *The Art of the Lands of the Bible*. New York: Atheneum Publishers, 1963. (U)

————. *The Art of the Eskimo*. New York: Harper & Row, Publishers, 1964. (U)

————. *The Art of Ancient Rome*. New York: Harper & Row, Publishers, 1965. (U)

————. *Art and Archeology*. New York: Harper & Row, Publishers, 1966. (U)

————. *The Art of the Etruscan*. New York: Harper & Row, Publishers, 1967. (U)

————. *The Art of the North American Indian*. New York: Harper & Row, Publishers, 1964. (U)

————. *The Art of Africa*. New York: Atheneum Publishers, 1965. (U)

————. *The Art of Ancient Peru*. New York: Atheneum Publishers, 1969. (U)

————. *The Art of India*. New York: The Macmillan Company, 1969. (U)

Gracza, Margaret. *The Ship and the Sea in Art*. Minneapolis: Lerner Publishing Co., 1964. (U)

————. *The Bird in Art*. Minneapolis: Lerner Publishing Co., 1965. (U)

Grossman, Mary Louise. *Birds of Prey of the World*. New York: Bonanza Books, 1969. (U)

Hammond, Penny, and Katrina Thomas. *My Skyscraper City*. Garden City, N. Y.: Doubleday & Company, Inc., 1963. (A)

Harkoven, Helen B. *Circuses and Fairs*. Minneapolis: Lerner Publishing Co., 1964. (U)

Hay, John, and Arline Strong. *A Sense of Nature*. Garden City, N. Y.: Doubleday & Company, Inc., 1962. (U)

Hellman Harold. *Art and Science of Color*. New York: McGraw-Hill Book Company, 1967. (U)

Herald, Earl S. *Living Fishes of the World*. Garden City, N. Y.: Doubleday & Company, Inc., 1961. (A)

Holme, Bryan. *Pictures to Live With*. New York: The Viking Press, Inc., 1959. (U)

————. *Drawings to Live With*. New York: The Viking Press, Inc., 1966. (U)

Janson, H. W., and D. J. Janson. *The Story of Painting for Young People*. New York: Harry N. Abrams, Inc., 1963. (U)

Kablo, Martin. *World of Color*. New York: McGraw-Hill Book Company, 1963. (P)

Katz, Herbert, and Marjorie Katz. *Museum Adventures*. New York: Coward-McCann, Inc., 1969. (U)

Kessler, Leonard. *Art Is Everywhere*. New York: Dodd, Mead & Co., 1958. (U)

————. *The Worm, The Bird and You*. New York: Dodd, Mead & Co., 1962. (A)

————. *What's in a Line?* New York: William R. Scott, Inc., 1961. (A)

Kirn, Ann. *Full of Wonder*. New York: World Publishing Company, 1959. (A)

Klots, A. B., and E. B. Klots. *Living Insects of the World.* Garden City, N. Y.: Doubleday & Company, Inc., 1959. (A)

Krauss, Ruth. *A Hole Is to Dig.* New York: Harper & Row, Publishers, 1952. (P)

Lerner, Sharon. *The Self-Portrait in Art.* Minneapolis: Lerner Publishing Co., 1964. (U)

Lewis, Richard. *Miracles.* Poems by Children. New York: Simon & Schuster, Inc., 1966. (U)

Linsenmaier, Walter. *Insects of the World.* New York: Time-Life Books, 1970. (A)

Lomel, Andreas. *The World of the Early Hunters.* London: Evelyn, Adams, and Mackay, 1967.

Low, Joseph. *Adam's Book of Odd Creatures.* New York: Atheneum Publishers, 1962. (A)

Moore, Janet Gaylord. *The Many Ways of Seeing.* New York: World Publishing Company, 1968. (U)

Munari, Bruno. *Bruno Munari's Zoo.* New York: World Publishing Company, 1963. (P)

Munro, Eleanor C. *The Golden Encyclopedia of Art.* New York: Golden Press, Inc., 1961. (U)

Nickel, Helmut. *Warriors and Worthies.* New York: Atheneum Publishers, 1969. (U)

O'Neill, Mary. *Hailstones and Halibut Bones.* Garden City, N. Y.: Doubleday & Company, Inc., 1961. (A)

Paine, Roberta M. *Looking at Sculpture.* New York: Lothrop, Lee & Shepard Co., Inc., 1968. (U)

Provensen, Alice. *What is Color?* New York: Golden Press, Inc., 1967. (U)

Reich, Hanns. *Horses.* New York: Hill & Wang, Inc., 1968. (U)

———. *Flight.* New York: Hill & Wang, Inc., 1963. (U)

———. *World from Above.* New York: Hill & Wang, Inc., 1967. (U)

———. *Baby Animals and Mothers.* New York: Hill & Wang, Inc., 1965. (A)

———. *Animals of Many Lands.* New York: Hill & Wang Inc., 1967. (A)

Ruskin, Ariane. *Story of Art for Young People.* New York: Pantheon Books, Inc., 1964. (U)

Sanderson, Ivan T. *Living Mammals of the World.* Garden City, N.Y.: Hanover House, 1955. (A)

Scheele, E. Wilham. *Prehistoric Animals.* New York: World Publishing Company, 1954. (U)

Schlein, Miriam. *Shapes.* New York: William R. Scott, Inc., 1958. (P)

Shissler, Barbara. *Sports and Games in Art.* Minneapolis: Lerner Publishing Co., 1965. (U)

Smith, William Jay. *What Did I See?* New York: Crowell, Collier Press and Macmillan, Inc., 1962. (P)

Strache, Wolf. *Forms and Patterns in Nature.* New York: Pantheon Books, Inc., 1956. (U)

Swinton, William Elgin. *The Wonderful World of Prehistoric Animals.* New York: Garden City Books, 1961. (U)

Weisgard, Leonard. *Treasures to See.* New York: Harcourt Brace Jovahovich, Inc., 1956. (U)

Wolff, Janet, and Bernard Owett. *Let's Imagine Colors.* New York: E. P. Dutton & Co., Inc., 1963. (A)

Wolff, Robert J. *Feeling Blue, Seeing Red, Hello, Yellow!* New York: Charles Scribner's Sons, 1968. (A)

Ylla. *Whose Eye Am I?* New York: Harper & Row, Publishers, 1969. (P)

Young, Mary. *Singing Windows.* The Stained Glass Wonder of Chartres. New York: Abingdon Press, 1962. (U)

Zuelke, Ruth. *The Horse in Art.* Minneapolis: Lerner Publishing Co., 1964. (U)

Life Nature Library. Morristown, N.J.: Silver Burdett Company.

The Plants   *The Fishes*
The Insects   *Animal Behavior*

BOOKS ON TEACHING ART

Cole, Natalie. *Children's Arts from Deep Down Inside.* New York: The John Day Co., Inc., 1966.

de Francesco, Italo L. *Art Education: Its Means and Ends.* New York: Harper & Row, Publishers, 1958.

Feldmand, Edmund Burke. *Becoming Human Through Art.* Englewood Cliffs, N.J.: Prentice-Hall, Inc., 1970.

Gaitskell, Charles D., and Al Hurwitz. *Children and Their Art.* New York: Harcourt Brace Jovanhovich, Inc., 1970.

Heberholz, Donald W., and Barbara Heberholz. *A Child's Pursuit of Art.* Dubuque, Iowa: William C. Brown Company, Publishers, 1969.

Kellogg, Rhoda, and Scott O'Dell. *Psychology of Children's Art.* New York: Random House, Inc., 1967.

Lansing, Kenneth. *Art, Artists and Art Education.* New York: McGraw-Hill Book Company, 1969.

Linderman, Earl W., and Donald W. Heberholz. *Developing Artistic and Perceptual Awareness.* Dubuque, Iowa: William C. Brown Company, Publishers, 1964.

Logan, Fred M. *Growth of Art in American Schools.* New York: Harper & Row, Publishers, 1955.

Lowenfeld, Viktor, and W. L. Brittain. *Creative and Mental Growth.* New York: The Macmillan Company, 1964.

Luca, Mark, and Robert Kent. *Art Education: Strategies of Teaching.* Englewood Cliffs, N. J.: Prentice-Hall, Inc., 1968.

McFee, June King. *Preparation for Art.* San Francisco: Wadsworth Publishing Co. Inc., 1961.

Merritt, Helen. *Guiding Free Expression in Children's Art.* New York: Holt, Rinehart & Winston, Inc., 1964.

Read, Herbert E. *Education Through Art.* New York: Pantheon Books, Inc., 1949.

Wachowiak, Frank, and David Hodge. *Art in Depth, A Qualitative Art Program for the Young Adolescent.* Scranton, Pa.: International Textbook Company, 1970.

BOOKS ON ART

Anderson, Donald M. *Elements of Design.* New York: Holt, Rinehart & Winston, Inc., 1961.

Bager, Bertel. *Nature as Designer.* New York: Van Nostrand Reinhold Company, 1966.

Bethers, Ray. *How Paintings Happen.* New York: W. W. Norton & Company, Inc., 1951.

————. *Composition in Pictures.* New York: Pitman Publishing Corp., 1956.

Canaday, John. *Keys to Art.* New York: Tudor Publishing Co., 1963.

Collier, Graham. *Form, Space and Vision.* Englewood Cliffs, N. J. Prentice-Hall, Inc., 1963.

Downer, Marion. *The Story of Design.* New York: Lothrop, Lee & Shepard Co., Inc., 1963.

Emerson, Sybil. *Design, A Creative Approach.* Scranton, Pa.: International Textbook Company, 1953.

Faulkner, R., E. Ziegfeld, and G. Hill. *Art Today.* New York: Holt, Rinehart & Winston, Inc., 1969.

Guyler, Vivian V. *Design in Nature.* Worcester, Mass.: Davis Publications, Inc., 1970.

Haberland, Wolfgang. *Art of North America.* New York: Crown Publishers, Inc., 1964.

Herold, Erich. *Tribal Masks: Art of Africa.* London: Paul Hamlyn, Ltd., 1967.

Hunt, K., and B. W. Carlson. *Masks and Mask Makers.* New York: Abingdon Press, 1961.

Kuh, Katherine. *Art Has Many Faces.* New York: Harper & Row, Publishers, 1951.

————. *The Artist's Voice.* New York: Harper & Row, Publishers, 1962.

Lowry, Bates. *The Visual Experience.* New York: Harry N. Abrams, Inc., 1961.

McIlhany, Sterling. *Art as Design: Design as Art.* New York: Van Nostrand Reinhold Company, 1970.

Moulin, Jean-Raoul. *Prehistoric Painting.* New York: Funk & Wagnalls, 1965.

Myers, Bernard S. *Art and Civilization.* New York: McGraw-Hill Book Company, 1967.

Ocvirk, Otto G., Robert Bone, Robert Stinson, and Philip Wigg. *Art Fundamentals: Theory and Practice.* Dubuque, Iowa: Wm. C. Brown Co., 1960.

Oeri, Georgine. *Man and His Images.* New York: The Viking Press, Inc., 1968.

Riley, Olive. *Masks and Magic.* New York: Studio Publications, Inc., 1955.

Rowland, Kurt. *Learning to See, Looking and Seeing.* New York: Van Nostrand Reinhold Company, 1970.

Schinneller, James A. *Art: Search and Self-Discovery.* Scranton, Pa.: International Textbook Company, 1969.

Schorr, Justin. *Aspects of Art.* Cranbury, N. J.: A. S. Barnes & Co., Inc., 1967.

BOOKS ON ART TECHNIQUES

Albert, Calvin, and Dorothy Seckler. *Figure Drawing Comes to Life.* New York: Van Nostrand Reinhold Company, 1962.

Andrews, Michael F. *Creative Printmaking.* Englewood Cliffs, N. J.: Prentice-Hall, Inc., 1963.

Argiro, Larry. *Mosaic Art Today.* Scranton, Pa.: International Textbook Company, 1961.

Beitler, Ethel Jane. *Create With Yarn.* Scranton, Pa.: International Textbook Company, 1964.

Cataldo, John W. *Lettering: A Guide for Teachers.* Worcester, Mass.: Davis Publications, Inc., 1958.

————. *Graphic Design and Visual Communications.* Scranton, Pa.: International Textbook Company, 1966.

————. *Words and Calligraphy for Children.* New York: Van Nostrand Reinhold Company, 1969.

Dhaemers, Robert, and Howard A. Slatoff. *Simple Jewelry Making for the Classroom.* Palo Alto, Cal.: Fearon Publishers, 1958.

Guild, Vera. *Creative Use of Stitches.* Worcester, Mass.: Davis Publications, Inc., 1964.

Horn, George F. *Bulletin Boards.* New York: Van Nostrand Reinhold Company, 1962.

————. *The Crayon.* Worcester, Mass.: Davis Publications, Inc., 1969.

Johnson, Pauline. *Creating with Paper.* Seattle: University of Washington Press, 1958.

Krevitsky, Nik. *Batik: Art and Craft.* New York: Van Nostrand Reinhold Company, 1964.

————. *Stitchery: Art and Craft.* New York: Van Nostrand Reinhold Company, 1966.

Lee, Ruth. *Exploring the World of Pottery.* Chicago: Children's Press, 1967.

Lidstone, John. *Building with Cardboard.* New York: Van Nostrand Reinhold Company, 1968.

Lynch, John. *How to Make Collages.* New York: The Viking Press, Inc., 1961.

Rainey, Sarita. *Weaving Without a Loom.* Worcester, Mass.: Davis Publications, Inc., 1966.

Randall, Reino, and Edward C. Haines. *Bulletin Boards and Display.* Worcester, Mass.: Davis Publications, Inc., 1961.

Rasmussen, Henry. *Printmaking with Monotype.* Philadelphia: Chilton Book Company, 1960.

Rottger, Ernst. *Creative Paper Design.* New York: Van Nostrand Reinhold Company, 1961.

————. *Creative Clay Design.* New York: Van Nostrand Reinhold Company, 1963.

Seidelman, James E. *The Rub Book.* New York: The Macmillan Company, 1968.

Untracht, Oppi. *Enameling on Metal.* New York: Greenberg Publishers, 1957.

Weiss, Harvey. *Clay, Wood and Wire.* New York: William R. Scott, Inc., 1956.

———. *Paper, Ink and Roller.* New York: William R. Scott, Inc., 1958.

———. *Pencil, Pen and Brush.* New York: William R. Scott, Inc., 1961.

———. *Sticks, Spools and Feathers.* New York: William R. Scott, Inc., 1962.

———. *Ceramics from Clay to Kiln.* New York: William R. Scott, Inc., 1964.

———. *Paint, Brush and Palette.* New York: William R. Scott, Inc., 1966.

PROFESSIONAL PUBLICATIONS

Films on Art
Slides and Filmstrips on Art
Planning Facilities for Art Instruction
Art Education in the Elementary School
Position Statements N.A.E.A.
Reproductions and Paper Backs on Art
Art Education for Elementary Teachers
   Washington, D. C.: National Art Education Association.
Gallery Book for Children, Marie Zoe Greene, Department of Education, The Art Institute of Chicago, Illinois.
Teacher's Idea Book, L. R. Kohls, Art Education Department, Des Moines Art Center, Iowa.
Zuga Kosaku (Arts and Crafts Guide for Japanese children. Graded Books 1-6), Nikon Bunkyo Shuppan, 4-15 Minami Sumiyoshi Sumiyoshi-Ku, Oska, Japan.

Colored construction paper lends itself well to many different kinds of art projects: a three-dimensional city (Grade 4), an expressive collage (Grade 1), or an Easter parade of rabbits (Grade 2).

233

CURRICULUM GUIDES

Education Through Art: Elementary School, Texas Education Agency, Austin, Texas.

Art in the Elementary Schools, New York City Board of Education.

Creative Art, Denver Public Schools, Denver, Colorado.

Children Learn and Grow Through Art Experiences, Bulletin C-4, State of Illinois Elementary Art Guide, Springfield, Illinois.

Art in Florida Elementary Schools, Bulletin 77, State Guide, Tallahassee, Florida.

Guidelines Art K-6, Kansas State Art Curriculum, Topeka, Kansas.

Art Education in Oregon Elementary Schools, Salem, Oregon.

Growth Through Art, City Elementary Art Guide, Milwaukee, Wisconsin.

Elementary Art Guide, State of Washington, Olympia, Washington.

Elementary Art Guide, State of Oklahoma, Oklahoma City, Oklahoma.

Art for Richmond's Children, City Elementary Art Guide, Richmond, Virginia.

PERIODICALS

Art Education, published October through June by the National Art Education Association, 1201 16th Street, N. W., Washington, D. C. 20036

Arts and Activities, published monthly except July and August by Publishers' Development Corporation, 8150 North Central Avenue, Skokie, Illinois. 60076

Ceramics Monthly, published monthly except July and August by Professional Publications, Inc., 4175 North High Street, Columbus, Ohio.

Craft Horizons, published bi-monthly by American Craftsmen's Council, 44 West 53rd Street, New York, New York. 10019

School Arts, published monthly September through June by the Davis Publications, Inc., Worcester, Massachusetts.

RESOURCE MAGAZINES

Audubon, Ebony, Eye, Family Circle, Harper's Bazaar, Holiday, House and Garden, House Beautiful, Ladies' Home Journal, Life, Look, McCall's, National Geographic, Natural History, Seventeen, Sports Illustrated, Sunset, Vogue, Woman's Day.

TOP—A plaster relief plaque. Objects used to make impressions in the clay negative mold included bent reed, marbles, wooden clothespins and beads, clock parts, cord, screw heads, and a ruler. OPPOSITE PAGE. LEFT—How expressively and perceptively this tree is drawn. Grade 6.

Japan. RIGHT—Examples of watercolor paintings by children in the primary grades. TOP and BOTTOM—Transparent watercolor (semimoist in tins) over permanent ink drawings. Grades 2 and 3, Iowa City, Iowa.

appendix

D

AUDIO VISUAL AIDS

FILMS

The letters following each film indicate whether suitable for primary grades (P), upper grades (U), and all grades (A). All films are 16 mm. sound and color. Distributors' addresses follow.

Alphabet in Art. Designing with letters. BFA (A)

Around my Way. New York City as seen through children's drawings. CON (U)

Art in Motion. Color and design in motion. EBF (U)

Art and Perception: Learning to See. BFA (A)

Arts and Crafts in West Africa. BFA (U)

Arts and Crafts of Mexico. EBF (U)

Artist and Nature. IFB (U)

Art in our World. BFA (U)

Art in Action with Dong Kingman. Shows the contemporary water colorist at work. HAR (U)

Art—What is it? Why is it? EBF (U)

Batik Rediscovered. BFA (U)

Begone Dull Care. Color patterns set to jazz music. IFB (A)

Behind the Scenes of a Museum. Visit to Chicago's Natural History Museum. IFB (U)

Birds and Etching. Simple engraving process. BFA (A)

Buma: African Sculpture Speaks. African masks. EBF (A)

Children Are Creative. Children in art activities. BFA (U)

Children Who Draw. Japanese children drawing and painting. BRAN (A)

Crayon Resist. Approaches to crayon resist. (A)

Creating with Clay. BFA (U)

Creating with Paper. BFA (A)

Design to Music. Children painting as mood music is played. IFB (A)

TOP—*Lino Print. Grade 5.* BOTTOM—*"Playing Ball." Grade 2.*

Discovering Art Series: Color; Composition; Creative Pattern; Dark and Light; Form in Art; Harmony in Art; Ideas in Art; Line; Texture. BFA (U)

Dots. Abstract designs set to music. IFB (A)

Eskimo Arts and Crafts. IFB (U)

Fiddle Dee Dee. Art abstractions accompanied by sprightly violin. IFB (A)

Indian Ceremonials. SF (U)

Insects and Painting. Child uses natural sources as inspiration for art. BFA (A)

Introduction to Sculpture Methods. Five sculptors in their studios. BFA (U)

Introduction to Contour Drawing. BFA (U)

Introduction to Gesture Drawing. BFA (U)

Introduction to Drawing Materials. BFA (U)

Japanese Handicrafts. BFA (U)

Junkyard. The junkyard as a visual and materials resource for art. BFA (U)

Lascaux: Cradle of Man's Art. The prehistoric cave paintings. IFB (A)

Look at that! Basic art elements through the eyes of two second graders. BFA (P)

Loon's Necklace. Tribal legend illustrated with North Pacific Indian masks. EBF (U)

Monotype Prints. Simple printmaking technique for primary grades. IFB (P)

Picture in Your Mind. IFB (U)

Rhythm and Movement in Art. BFA (U)

Sun Symbol in Art. Fourth graders create sun images. BFA (U)

The Sumi Artist. Japanese brush painting techniques. LOB (U)

Torn Paper. Simple torn paper technique. IFB (A)

Totems. Tree carvings by Indians of British Columbia. IFB (U)

Trip to the Moon. Children of many countries paint their interpretations of a moon shot. BRAN (U)

Van Gogh. Folk song narrative accompanies showing of this artists paintings. BFA (U)

Watts Towers. Colorful filming of Simon Rodia's fantastic structure in Watts, California. CFS (A)

Weeds and Mosaics. Simple mosaic and collage techniques utilizing found items. BFA (U)

What Shall We Paint. BFA (U)

FILM DISTRIBUTORS

BFA	BFA Educational Media, 11559 Santa Monica Blvd., Los Angeles, Calif. 90025.
BRAN	Brandon Films, Inc., 221 West 57th Street, New York, N. Y. 10019.
CFS	Creative Film Society, 14558 Valerio, Van Nuys, Calif. 91405.
CON	Contemporary Films, Inc., 330 West 42nd Street, New York, N. Y. 10036.
EBF	Encyclopedia Britannica Films, 425 N. Michigan Avenue, Chicago, Ill. 60611.
HAR	Harmon Foundations, 140 Nassau Street, New York, N. Y. 10038.
IFB	International Film Bureau, Inc., 332 South Michigan Avenue, Chicago, Ill. 60604.
LOB	Lobett Productions, 2002 Taraval Street, San Francisco, Calif.
SF	Santa Fe Film Bureau, 80 E. Jackson Blvd., Chicago, Ill. 60604.

College and university instructors of art education courses and art education workshop consultants may be interested to know that two color filmstrips based on "Emphasis: Art" projects are available from International Film Bureau Inc., Chicago, Illinois.

appendix

E

ART MATERIALS AND SOURCES

RECYCLING FOUND MATERIALS

When teachers consider supplies for art activities, they generally think first in terms of those materials that are available on the commercial art market. In today's productive world, however, there are a number of other sources they should tap, among them the discarded or junked everyday items, empty packages, scraps, remnants, and a hundred other things ordinarily thought of as worthless but that with a little imagination can be recycled into the art program.

Most of the items listed on the following pages can be found in basements, attics, garages, alleys, junkyards, store disposal areas, and waste baskets. Children and their parents should be enlisted in the campaign to build a store of discarded items, remnants, and *found objects*.

Shopping bags, shoe boxes, cigar boxes, and gallon ice cream cartons can serve as containers for the accumulated materials. *Found objects* can definitely enrich and expand the elementary art program especially when the school is operating on a limited budget. However, both teacher and students must use discrimination and restraint to prevent the *found materials* from winding up in *lost results*.

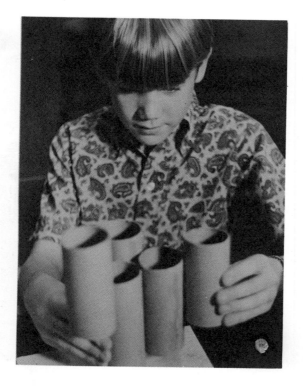

TOP—Lino Print. Grade 5. BOTTOM—Youngster uses discarded cardboard tubes to construct a space design.

238

Material	Use	Material	Use
Asbestos, powdered	Mix with wheat paste for modeling	Boxes, cardboard	Box sculpture; masks; storage for *found materials;* display stands
Baby food jars	Paint containers; containers for melted crayon	Boxes, cigar	Storage; box sculpture; bases and display stands
Bags, paper	Masks; storage of *found materials*	Boxes, oatmeal (round)	Box sculpture; foundations for construction; paper totem poles
Balloons	Foundations for papier-mâché, paper sculpture, or clay slab pots	Boxes, suit or dress	Cardboard constructions; collographs; mobiles
Balls, rubber, styrofoam, ping pong	3-D construction, mobiles	Buckles (metal)	Imprinting in clay
Bamboo shade sticks	3-D construction; collage; ink-drawing tool	Buckram	Collage, collograph
		Bulbs, electric light	Foundations for puppet heads
Bark	Collage; rubbings		
Beads	Construction; collage	Bulbs, photoflash	Imprinting in clay
Blades, razor (single-edge)	Cutting and crayon engraving tool. Use caution.	Buttons	Collage; constructions; imprinting in clay
Blades, saw	Make textures in clay or dry plaster	Candles	Resist paintings; encaustic painting
Blinds, matchstick	Collage; 3-D construction; ink-drawing tool	Cans, tin	Water, crayon, or paint containers
Blocks (wood)	Bases for sculpture; constructions	Canvas	Collage; collograph; surface for clay wedging or slab-making
Blotters	Collage	Caps (bottle)	Collage; imprinting in clay
Bolts and nuts	Imprinting in clay	Cards, game	Collage; 3-D constructions; mobiles
Bones	Imprinting in clay; 3-D construction	Cardboard, corrugated	Collage; collograph; rubbings; paper sculpture
Book jackets	Tesserae for paper mosaic; collage; montage	Carpet samples	Collage
		Cartons, egg	Collage; box sculpture; masks
Bottles (colored)	Broken pieces for mosaics, stained glass windows, plaster reliefs	Cartons, milk (qt, ½ gal)	Plaster carving block mold

MATERIAL	USE	MATERIAL	USE
Cartons, milk (½ pint)	Tempera paint containers. Can be sealed with clothespin or plastic clamps	Contact paper (transparent)	Protective covering for resource pictures and reproductions
Cartons, ice cream (round)	Plaster carving mold container; storage of *found materials*	Cord	Collage; imprinting in clay
		Corks	Collage; construction in 3-D; mobiles; imprinting in clay
Cellophane (colored)	Light mobiles; color modulators; color windows	Corn cobs	Imprinting on clay
		Cotton warp	Stitchery; collage
Cellulose sponges	Printmaking; painting; clean-up	Cups (paper)	Paper and box sculpture
		Dental tools	Engraving tools
Celotex	Working surface for bent reed constructions	Dominoes	Collage; constructions; imprinting in clay
Chains (metal)	Imprinting in clay	Drapery samples	Collage; crafts
Checkers	Constructions; imprinting in clay	Driftwood	Still-life arrangements
		Embroidery hoops	Simple screen printmaking
Clips, paper	Collage; imprinting in clay	Emery cloth	Collage
Clock mechanism parts	Collage; imprinting in clay	Feathers	Collage; imprinting in clay; rubbings
Cloth, terry or cheese	Staining or applying patina to clay, papier-mâché or plaster sculpture	Felt	Collage; stitchery and appliqué
Coins	Collage; imprinting in clay	Filler, rug	Stitchery and appliqué; collage
Combs	Crayon engraving; imprinting in clay	Fish net	Collage; still-life material
		Flour	Papier-mâché; salt and flour modeling paste
Cones, fir	Imprinting in clay	Flowers (dried)	Still-life material
Cones, paper	Paper sculpture	Foam rubber (discards)	Collage; 3-D construction
Confetti	Collage; paper sculpture decoration	Foil, aluminum	Metal repoussé; collage; collograph embellishment
		Foil, aluminum (heavy duty)	Crinkle into shape for a plaster mold

MATERIAL	USE	MATERIAL	USE
Fur	Collage; 3-D construction	Paper towels	Papier-mâché; collage; collograph; blotting tempera batiks
Gourds	Still-life material; imprinting in clay		
Grog	Aggregate for plaster molds; clay conditioner	Paper (wrapping, shelf)	Tempera painting surface; printmaking; fingerpainting; collage; collograph
Keys	Collage; imprinting in clay	Pebbles and stones	Plaster reliefs; ceramic display; imprinting in clay; collage
Lath, wire	Imprinting in clay		
Leather	Collage; collograph; tooling		
Leaves (plastic)	Still-life material; stenciling; imprinting in clay	Pegboard (discards)	Collage; 3-D constructions; storage; display
Linoleum (discards)	Printmaking; collage; rubbings; collograph	Periodicals (magazines)	Pasting surfaces
		Pins	Multiple purposes
Machine parts	Imprinting in clay reliefs	Pipe cleaners	Collage; miniature armatures; crafts
Magazines	Collage; mosaics; pasting surface; source material	Plastic (discards)	Metal sculpture; mobiles; collage
Marbles	Imprinting in clay	Plywood (discards)	Collage; 3-D constructions; bases for sculpture
Masonite (discards)	Collage; inking surfaces; 3-D constructions		
Mats, floor (rubber)	Collage; collograph	Polish (furniture, shoe)	Staining plaster, gesso-coated papier-mâché and clay
Mirrors (broken)	Mosaics		
Nails	Engraving; imprinting in clay	Q-tips	Applying melted crayon in encaustic; applying stains
Newspapers	Multiple purposes; padding for crayon application	Raffia	Hair for masks or puppets; collage
Nut picks	Engraving tools	Reed	3-D construction; collage; imprinting in clay
Oilcloth	Surface for clay and finger-painting projects	Ribbon, ric rac	Collage; stitchery and appliqué
Paint (leftovers)	Painting projects, murals	Rope	Collage; 3-D construction; imprinting in clay; display
Paper trays, plates	Masks; box sculpture		

Material	Use	Material	Use
Rubber, tire innertube	Collage; collograph	Tins (baby food)	Containers to melt crayon in encaustic process; tempera paint containers
Rug (remnants, samples)	Collage; texture printing		
Salt	Salt and flour modeling paste	Tins (pie, cookie)	Paint mixing palettes or containers
Sandpaper	Collage; surface for melted crayon pictures; collograph	Tongue depressors	Collage; paint stirring sticks; 3-D construction
Screws (metal)	Imprinting in clay	Toothbrushes	To clean recessed areas in plaster sculpture and relief
Sea shells	Still-life material; imprinting in clay		
Shades, window	Collage; collograph; painting or printmaking surface	Toothpicks	3-D construction; collage; collograph; applying glue
		Tubes (mailing)	Box sculpture
Shingles (tar, wood)	Collage; collograph; 3-D construction; rubbings	TV dinner trays	Paint mixing palettes; metal sculpture and reliefs
Skull, animal	Still-life material	Vermiculite	Aggregate for plaster; collage
Sponge (metal, plastic)	Imprinting in clay		
Spools (thread)	Box sculpture; 3-D constructions; imprinting in clay	Wallpaper (samples)	Collage; rubbings; painting, printmaking surface
Steel wool	Cleaning and burnishing metal; imprinting in clay	Wax (liquid)	Coating for stained clay, tempera batiks, papier-mâché, wood sculpture, and reliefs
Sticks (applicator, paste, pick-up)	3-D constructions; collage		
Straws (wax, cellophane, paper)	3-D constructions; mobiles	Weeds	Still-life material
		Wood (assorted)	Wood sculpture and reliefs; printmaking; bases for sculpture
Tarpaper	Collage; collograph		
Tile (acoustic)	Collage; 3-D constructions; bases space modulators	X-ray plates (used)	Collage; printmaking plate in engravings
Tile (vinyl)	Collage; collograph; inking surface	Yarn	Stitchery, appliqué, collage

SPECIAL MATERIALS AND TOOLS: SUGGESTED USES, SOURCES

MATERIAL	USE	SOURCE
Aggregate (vermiculite)	Mix with plaster to make mold for carving	Builder's supply
Applicator sticks (wood)	Constructions; stabiles; mobiles; collage	Drug store, hospital supply
Artape (assorted colors)	Collage; design projects	Art and craft supply
Baren (hand press)	Printmaking	Art supply
Beaverboard (Upson Board)	Drawing or sketching boards; desk and table protection; mural background surface	Builder's supply
Brayer (rubber roller)	Printmaking; inking plate	Art supply
Burlap (assorted colors)	Stitchery; appliqués; display	Department store
Celotex (scraps)	Working surface for reed, stick, or straw constructions; also serves as base	Builder's supply
Cement (Testor Formula AA)	Fast-drying adhesive for reed, sticks, drinking straw constructions	Art and craft supply
Contact paper (transparent)	Protective surface for resource pictures; backing for stained-glass designs	Department store
Craypas	Combination crayon and oil medium for picturemaking	Art supply
Dextrin (powdered)	Add to dry or moist clay (5% to 10%) and finished pieces will harden without firing	Drug supply
Duco cement	Construction and collage	Art and craft supply
Easycurve Board	Sturdy yet pliable cardboard for constructions and display	Builder's supply
Elmer's Glue	Constructions; collage; monoprinting; sealing surfaces	Art and craft supply
Featherock	Lightweight, gray porous pumice for carving	Art and craft supply
Firebrick	Lightweight, porous refractory brick for carving	Builder's or ceramic supply
Foamglass	Light, black, porous block for upper-level carving projects	Pittsburg Plate Glass Company
Gesso	A liquid for coating papier-mâché constructions	Art and craft supply
Masonite (tempered)	Clay boards; inking surfaces; rinsing surfaces for tempera batik process	Builder's supply

MATERIAL	USE	SOURCE
Mat knife	Cutting mats, mounts; cardboard construction	Art and craft supply
Modpodge	Collage, decoupage, montage	Art and craft supply
Pariscraft	Plaster-impregnated gauze in varied width strips for sculpture projects	Art and craft supply
Pentel	Oil pastels for painting and picture making	Art and craft supply
Plaster (molding)	Carving molds; reliefs; applied sculpture	Builder's supply
Polymer medium	Painting vehicle especially used for glazing; may be diluted with water	Art and craft supply
Polytemps	Tempera in cake form	Art and craft supply
Printing press	Sturdy press for acetate or cardboard engravings	Laszlo Universal or Printmaster
P.V.A. (Poly Vinyl Acetate)	Adhesive for plastics, glass, tile	Art and craft supply
Railroad board	In assorted colors for multicrayon engraving surface	Art and craft supply
Reed (round)	For stabiles; mobiles; space modulators	Art and craft supply
Reeve's cakes	Opaque watercolor in cake form	Art and craft supply
Rub 'n' Buff	Metallic finishes and patinas in paste form for sculpture, reliefs, ceramics	Art and craft supply
Sculpmetal	Metal finishes in paste form for sculpture and jewelry	Art and craft supply
Sculpstone	Carving material	Art and craft supply
Shreddimix	Prepared mixture for papier-mâché projects	Art and craft supply
Sigment	Strong fast-drying cement for constructions and crafts	Art and craft supply
Sloyd knife	Utility knife with 2-inch semi-sharp blade for carving in sculpture, engraving processes.	Art and craft supply
Tidy tubs	Tempera paint in cake form	Art and craft supply
Tongue depressors	Wooden paddles for mixing paint	Drug supply
Transfer paper	White dressmaker's carbon for transferring sketches to black surfaces as in crayon engravings	Singer Company

MATERIAL	USE	SOURCE
Wilhold	White liquid glue for adhering purposes in collage, constructions; also for glue relief prints	Art and craft supply
Wood stains	Stains in walnut, mahogany, and oak for glazing ceramic pieces, plaster sculpture and reliefs, and gesso-coated papier-mâché creations	Paint store
X-Acto knife	Craft knife with interchangeable blades for cutting cardboard	Art and craft supply

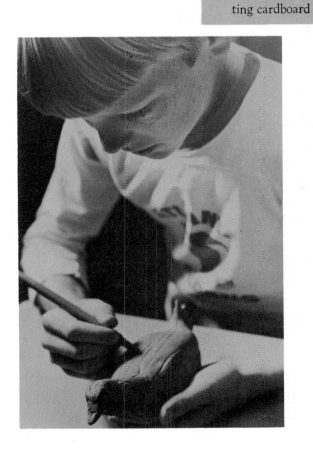

appendix

F

FACILITIES FOR ART

The qualitative art program in the elementary school depends, in part, on adequate and functional instructional facilities. Some schools boast a multipurpose art room, but the majority of elementary art experiences today take place in the contained classroom. This often places a limitation on the variety of art activities that can be programmed. However, if certain minimal and vital art facility requirements are met in the plans of the classrooms still to be constructed, the climate for growth in art in tomorrow's elementary schools will be a more favorable one. Basically the changes that need to be made are in the strategic areas of storage, display, and clean-up.

LOCATION

If a multipurpose art room is planned, it should be preferably on the first or ground floor, adjacent to the stage of the auditorium or to the cafeteria and near a service entrance. An outdoor court, easily accessible from the art room, can provide excellent auxiliary space for sketching, mural making, ceramics, constructions, and sculptural projects in favorable weather.

OPPOSITE PAGE—Illustrations show easily constructed storage units and paint cart. Children's art gains prestige and needed support from the public when it is displayed effectively and tastefully in schools or art centers. THIS PAGE. TOP—Lino Print. Grade 3. BOTTOM—Self-portrait. Black and white crayon on gray manila paper. Grade 4.

SPACE ALLOTMENT

Enough space should be provided to allow students to work on individual projects with some flexibility of movement, to permit rearrangement of furniture for group projects, and to insure a regular flow of student traffic to storage, display, and clean-up areas or stations.

The self-contained classroom should be planned to provide adequate space at the rear of the room and along one or two walls for storage, clean-up (sink) facility, and counter or surface working areas. There should be sufficient room at the rear of the class for one or more large tables for group projects or special craft activities.

FURNITURE

In both the self-contained classroom or the special art room, desk and table surfaces of nonglare, waterproof, and scratch-resistant material are recommended. White formica working surfaces have many advantages but they must be protected during projects involving cutting or hammering. Tables and desks should be adjustable for height and easily movable to provide for group or project activities. In the multipurpose art room, stools which can be recessed under tables can ease the traffic problem. In the primary-level classrooms free-standing easels can effectively augment the limited table and desk painting surface.

STORAGE

Effective storage facilities are a definite asset in expediting a qualitative art program. There should be adequate storage for art supplies, tools, visual aids, projects in process, and completed art work reserved for display.

Supply storage should be provided for assorted art papers (drawers or slots should have inside measurements slightly larger than the size of the paper itself); tempera or poster paint, watercolors, oil pastels, crayons, inks, paste (adjustable shelves are recommended for these supplies); yarn, wood, *found materials,* clay (bin type storage, tote-tray cabinet, mobile metal-lined clay cart, galvanized or heavy plastic waste containers, large cardboard cartons painted in bright colors).

A cabinet or movable cart with shelves and panels is suggested for small tool storage. A simple pegboard panel attached to a wall and the necessary accompanying hardware will alleviate the most pressing tool storage problems. Painting an identifying shape or outline of each tool on the panel will help expedite storage and provide a ready inventory of tools.

Since so much of the children's art centers around painting, there should be adequate horizontal storage spaces for painting projects in process. This is especially true in the special art room where one class follows another and painting stations must be cleared quickly. There are some excellent horizontal storage facilities on the art market but too often the budget does not allow for their purchase. A simple yet effective flatwork storage unit can be constructed of a strong framework of ¾-inch plywood (one side finished) and pull-out shelves of masonite, plywood, or ⅜-inch Upsonboard. A clothesline and spring clothespins can be used as a drying facility for in-process and completed vegetable, cardboard, or linoleum prints.

A critical problem in the self-contained classroom is the storage of three-dimensional projects in process such as clay sculpture or pottery, paper sculpture, papier-mâché or box constructions, stabiles, and mobiles. Counter space above storage cabinets, the floor along a wall, and closet shelves are some possibilities. Tote trays provide another solution. Mobiles in process or on display could be suspended from a wire line strung from the tops of doors and windows. Avoid hanging mobiles and other constructions from light fixtures or light baffles. This practice may prove hazardous and damaging.

CLEAN-UP FACILITIES

In order to minimize traffic problems, the sink or sinks should be easily accessible from all parts of the classroom. They should not be located in a closet or a corner of the room. They should be stainproof and clean with ease. Multiple mixing faucets and heavy duty drains and sink traps are recommended. Sinks

should be large enough to allow several youngsters to use them at the same time. They should be low enough so that the children can reach them with ease; if not, they should be provided with step-up platforms. For special art rooms a peninsula or island sink is recommended.

DISPLAY FACILITIES

A generous amount of space should be allotted for display purpose and for instructional bulletin boards. This holds true for either the special art room or the self-contained classroom. Display and exhibition panel backgrounds should be neutral in color. Subtle nonglare whites, grays, and blacks are recommended. Use bold colors with caution. Surfaces, in most instances, should be soft, matte finish with easy pinning or stapling properties such as cork or cloth-covered celotex. Random-punch butt-end acoustic tile can be glued directly to wall surfaces or to masonite panels to form a simple, yet effective, display facility. Cork-surfaced doors on cupboards and storage cabinets will augment the display possibilities. In the newest art rooms cork display panels from floor to ceiling are being installed. It is advisable in future school planning to reserve one classroom wall entirely for display or mural-making surfaces. Recessed cabinets, with sliding glass doors and directed spot-lighting, both in classrooms and hallways, can add immeasurably to the effective display space for many three-dimensional projects and crafts.

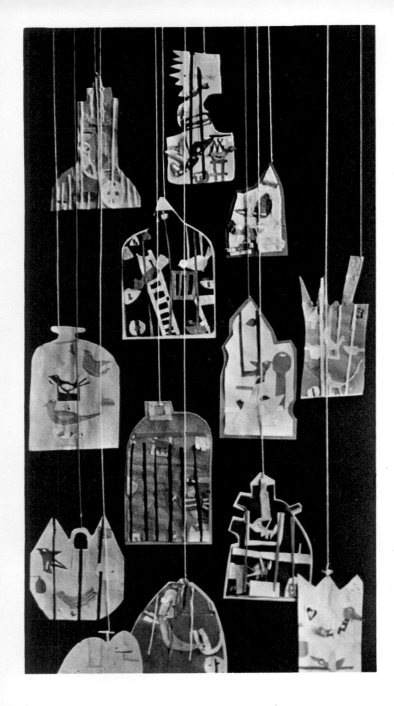

OTHER SPECIFICATIONS

Floors should be of nonskid material, hard, yet resilient and easily cleaned. Neutral colored asphalt or plastic tile is generally recommended. Ceilings should be acoustically treated and of a bright color that provides maximum light reflection. Lighting should be of sufficient kilowatt intensity to provide students with adequate light and minimum glare. Room-darkening shades or blinds should be installed to expedite the showing of color slides and films. White-surfaced slate boards can aid effectively in presenting art lessons in a more realistic context. These boards can also serve as screens for slide and film projection. Electric outlets should be provided at intervals around the classroom. Check with the electrician on voltage needed especially if a clay or enamel kiln is to be installed. Electrical outlets should not be adjacent to sink areas.

SPECIAL EQUIPMENT

Whether in the self-contained classroom or the art room, special furniture and equipment can often be a deciding factor in implementing the program. The following items are generally recommended: clay bin or cart, vibrating jig saw, heavy-duty clothes wringer, color-slide projector, projection screen, workbench with vises, large-size paper cutter, electric heating plate, utility cart, ceramic kiln, metal enameling kiln, free-standing easels, drying rack for flat work in progress, gun tacker, stapler.

Each youngster contributed his own individually constructed birds and cage to this panel of cages tied together by colored yarn. Colored construction paper collage. Grade 1.

appendix

G

GLOSSARY

Abstract art—a visual interpretation that expresses the essence of a figure, object, or place in lines, geometric forms, or planes with little regard for its natural appearance.

Acetone—a solvent for plastics.

Aesthetic—appreciative of, or responsive to, the beautiful in art or nature.

Alcohol—a solvent for shellac (methanol or shellacol).

Armature—framework used to support modeling substances such as clay, papier-mâché or plaster (usually constructed of wood, plastic, metal, or wire mesh).

Assemblage—contemporary art expression which utilizes *found materials* in a combination of collage, painting, and sculptural relief.

Asymmetric—a balance in art composition based on informal relationships.

Balsa—a strong, lightweight wood for carving, constructions, model building, and collages.

Baren—a device made of cardboard and dried leaf which is used as a hand press for taking a print.

Bas-relief—low relief (the opposite of incised relief).

Bat—a flat, level-surfaced plaster slab used to absorb moisture from wet clay (a bat can be cast by pouring wet plaster into a vaseline-coated round plastic dishpan).

Batik—a method of designing on fabric by sealing with wax those areas not to be colored by the liquid dye (term also used to describe crayon and tempera resist techniques).

Bisque—unglazed pottery after first firing. (also *biscuit*)

Bit—a tool used with a brace for drilling or boring.

TOP—Lino Print. Grade 4, Japan. BOTTOM—Only in clay could a child capture the quality of this delightful figure. Grade 2.

251

Brayer—rubber roller used in inking printing plates or blocks and sometimes as a pressure roller for taking print (softer gelatin brayers are also available for collographs, monoprinting, and brayer painting).

Burnish—to make smooth or shiny by a rubbing or polishing action.

Burr—a rough ridge in metal, clay, or other substance created by a gouging tool passing through the surface area.

Calligraphy—beautiful handwriting or penmanship. A script, usually cursive, produced by brush and ink.

Center of interest—that part of a picture or composition first to attract attention.

Charcoal—drawing stick or pencil of blackened charred wood.

Chipboard—heavy cardboard, usually gray, in various thicknesses for collage, construction, and collographs.

Chroma—another designation for color or hue.

Collage—composition made by assembling, pasting, and gluing materials to a flat surface (can be combined with drawing, painting, and glazing).

Collograph—a print made from a collaged surface created with assorted weight cardboards, tapes, string, glue, and papers.

Colors: *Primary*—red, yellow, blue; three basic hues which cannot be produced by a mixture of other hues.

Secondary—orange, green, purple; colors achieved by mixing the primaries.

Tertiary—colors derived by mixing the secondaries: red-orange, blue-green, etc., sometimes called intermediate hues.

Analogous—colors closely related, neighbors on the color wheel; yellow, orange, pink, red, for example.

Complementary—colors opposite each other on the color wheel; sharply contrasting colors.

Triad—colors equidistant from each other on the color wheel.

Warm—colors usually associated with fire, the sun, the earth; red, brown, orange, yellow, umber, sienna, ochre.

Cool—colors usually associated with water, the sky, and foliage; green, blue, turquoise, chartreuse.

Contour drawing—a line drawing delineating the external boundaries of a shape or form.

Crosshatch—create darker values in a linear composition by using sets of parallel lines that cross each other. (also *hatching*)

Design—an ordered arrangement of one or more of the components of art: line, value, shape, form, or color.

Dowel—a thin cylinder of wood available in graded dimensions for constructions and crafts.

Embossing—raising a surface of metal or leather in relief (*tooling*).

Empathy—the projection of one's personality into the object of contemplation; a feeling into.

Emphasis—a principle in design or composition which establishes importance or significance. It often implies subordinate and dominant elements or areas.

Encaustic—a painting technique in which pigments mixed with beeswax are applied to a surface. Sometimes used to describe melted crayon processes.

Engobe—liquid clay or slip applied as color for surface decoration in ceramics; apply while clay is moist.

Engraving—the process of incising or scratching into metal or other prepared surfaces with a sharp tool.

Expression—in art, a subjective interpretation of sensations, emotions, or ideas rather than of actual appearances.

Finding—metal clasps, loops, etc. used on jewelry.

Fixative—a commercial preparation in liquid or spray form used to protect easily-smudged surfaces such as chalk pastel. Also *fixatif*.

Flux—a material applied to a point to be soldered to prevent oxides from forming when the metal is heated.

Focal point—a point or spot of interest in a composition where the beholder's eye comes to rest.

Foot—in ceramics, the foot of a pot or container.

Foreshortening—the apparent visual compression or distortion of forms in a composition to indicate depth in space.

Form—usually a sculptural or three-dimensional shape defined by its characteristic contour.

Found materials—discards, remnants, samples, leftovers, etc. for use in collages, assemblages, constructions. Anything found on a walk such as a shell, driftwood, etc.

Frottage—a design created by rubbing. A thin, flexible paper is placed over an object (preferably textured) and rubbed with pencil, wax or conte crayon, or oil pastel until an image appears. Rubbings may also be made of collages, incised reliefs, woodblocks, collograph plates, etc.

Genre—compositions which emphasize everyday events.

Gesso—a dense and brilliantly white ground used in oil painting. Can be applied to papier-mâché as a surface for further painting.

Glaze—a transparent or partly transparent surface finish for oil painting; also for sculpture or plaster relief embellishment; opaque glazes available for ceramic ware.

Glazing—the process of applying a transparent layer of paint over a solid or opaque one so that the color of the first layer is modified.

Greenware—unfired ceramic ware; leather-hard stage, when clay is firm but not quite fully dry.

Grog—fired clay ground to a powder; provides porosity and texture in clay pieces to be fired.

Ground—the surface on which a painting is made.

Horizon line—an imaginary line, usually at the eye level of the observer, where the sky seems to meet the earth.

Hue—color or chroma.

Impasto—a particularly thick or heavy application of paint.

Intaglio—an engraved design (the opposite of relief).

Intensity—in reference to color, the brightness or dullness.

Kiln—an oven or furnace for drying, firing, and glazing ceramic or metal-enameled ware (pronounced "kill").

Kiln wash—a protective coating that prevents excessive glaze from sticking to kiln shelves.

Kneaded eraser—soft workable eraser for charcoal drawing.

Line—a mark made by a moving point.

Linear composition—a composition or design whose effectiveness depends on the pattern made by the outlines of the shapes or forms represented rather than on the mass of tone, value, or color.

Local color—the positive or natural color of an object or element; for example, leaf-green, lemon-yellow, sky-blue.

Masonite—a pressed board made of wood fibers. Recommended for clay boards, table tops, and inking surfaces.

Mass—a large form or substantial area of color or value.

Mat board—a heavy poster used for mounting or matting pictures. Sometimes board is textured.

Matte (mat)—a term describing a dull, flat, nonglossy surface.

Medium—any material used for art expression, such as clay, paint, crayon, wood, or metal.

Middle ground—that part of a painting or picture halfway between spectator and background.

Mixed medium—a term describing art work made up of mixed materials or techniques.

Monoprint—a type of surface printmaking in which the design is created on a hard surface such as glass or formica with oil, ink, or fingerpaint, usually scratching through the ink, oil, or paint for linear effects and then transferring the design to a paper pressed over the surface of the glass.

Montage—a kind of collage created with many heterogeneous pieces of photos or pictures overlapping each other.

Mosaic—a design or composition formed by the planned juxtaposition of clay or glass tesserae cemented in grout or mortar. Also refers to mosaics made of colored paper.

Motif—center or dominant theme or feature in a design or composition.

Mural—a wall painting or composition usually performing an architectonic function. May also be executed as a ceramic design, metal repoussé, or collage.

Oil pastel—combines qualities of oil and chalk pastel.

Papier-mâché—a substance made of paper pulp conditioned with sizing or paste.

Pastel—another name for soft colored chalk sticks; also a description for the tints of colors.

Patina—the greenish incrustation on the surface of old bronze. Also the term used to describe the staining of ceramic or plaster creations with polymer or metallic finishes.

Perspective—the representation of three-dimensional objects in spatial recession on a two-dimensional surface.

Plaster (moulding)—a white powdery substance which, when mixed with water, forms a quick-setting casting or construction material; also used for molds, clay bats, etc.

Positive-negative—positive areas in a composition or design are the objective shapes and forms; negative areas usually refer to the unoccupied or empty spaces.

Pyrometric cones—clay cones which melt at different temperatures to measure the heat in a kiln.

Proportion—the relation of one part to a whole or to other parts.

Radiation—divergent lines, shapes, or colors emanating from a central point of interest.

Raffia—a palm fiber available in a wide range of colors for use in weaving and constructions.

Relief—sculpture which is not free-standing. Also may refer to constructed reliefs in cardboard, and in other materials. See bas and incised relief.

Repoussé—metal work in which the design or decoration is hammered into a bas relief form from the reverse side.

Rhythm—an ordered movement created by the repetition of pictorial or design elements.

Rubber cement—a clean, quick-drying latex type of cement or glue.

Scoring—to mark with grooves, using an edged tool, as a preliminary step to cementing clay parts or as a guide for folding in paper sculpture.

Shape—area, form, or mass with a specific character and often defined by outline or contrast.

Slip—clay mixed with water to consistency of cream. Used like glue to adhere pieces or surfaces of clay together. Also used in clay decoration.

Solvent—a liquid which dissolves or reduces the viscosity of other liquids; for example, turpentine is solvent for oil paint, alcohol is solvent for shellac.

Space: three-dimensional—in art, a structure or form possessing thickness or depth as well as length and breadth.

Stabile—a design in space usually made of wire, sticks, string, and other affinitive materials mounted on a base and having no moving parts (*space modulator*).

Symbol—in art, the representation of an object, idea, or quality through an intermediate figure, sign, or geometric character.

Tempera—an opaque, water-soluble paint in which pigment is mixed with albuminous material. Available in powder or liquid form. Also called poster paint.

Terra cotta—an earth-colored clay, generally unglazed.

Tessera—a small, geometric segment of glass, marble, stone, or similar material used in mosaic techniques.

Texture—the actual and/or visual feel of a surface; the representation of the tactile character of a given material or substance.

Tie and dye—a fabric design technique in which cloth is tied in knots or tied with string and then immersed in dye colors.

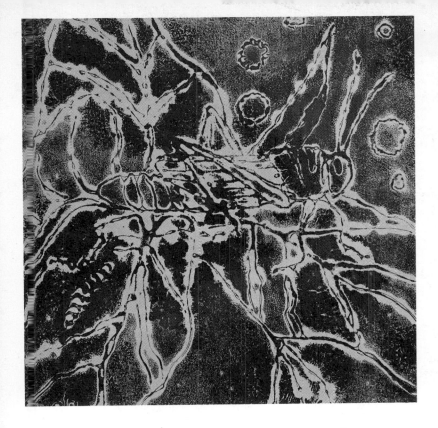

Tint—a graduation of a color achieved by mixing it with white pigment or diluting it with a solvent. Also a designation for the light values of a color.

Translucent—semi-opaque, partly transparent.

Value—an attribute of color, its lightness or darkness; for example, values of red might range from pink to maroon.

Vanishing point—in perspective drawing, a point or points to which all lines recede.

Vermiculite—a form of insulation material generally used as an aggregate in plaster carving molds.

Wash—a thinly applied paint usually found in watercolor techniques.

Wedging—a method of preparing clay by kneading it to expel air pockets and make it constantly plastic.

Welding—in clay modeling, the process of adhering two pieces of clay with slip and/or scoring procedures.

X-ray picture—in children's art, the unique interpretation of places normally hidden from view; for example, a coal mine, a gopher's home, a tunnel under a river, an aquanaut station undersea.

Glue relief prints created by elementary teachers at an inservice workshop sponsored by the Bibb County Services Center, Macon, Georgia. Teachers were motivated by color slides and color study photos on insects and fish from the Society for Visual Education, Inc., 1345 Diversey Parkway, Chicago. Size of prints: 12" x 12".